PENGUIN BOOKS

Can't Anyone Help Me?

Can't Anyone Help Me?

JACKIE HOLMES WITH
TONI MAGUIRE

PENGUIN BOOKS

PENGUIN BOOKS

Published by the Penguin Group
Penguin Books Ltd, 80 Strand, London WC2R ORL, England
Penguin Group (USA) Inc., 375 Hudson Street, New York, New York 10014, USA
Penguin Group (Canada), 90 Eglinton Avenue East, Suite 700, Toronto, Ontario, Canada M4P 2Y3
(a division of Pearson Penguin Canada Inc.)
Penguin Ireland, 25 St Stephen's Green, Dublin 2, Ireland (a division of Penguin Books Ltd)
Penguin Group (Australia), 250 Camberwell Road,
Camberwell, Victoria 3124, Australia (a division of Pearson Australia Group Pty Ltd)
Penguin Books India Pvt Ltd, 11 Community Centre,
Panchsheel Park, New Delhi – 110 017, India
Penguin Group (NZ), 67 Apollo Drive, Rosedale, Auckland 0632, New Zealand
(a division of Pearson New Zealand Ltd)
Penguin Books (South Africa) (Pty) Ltd, 24 Sturdee Avenue,
Rosebank, Johannesburg 2196, South Africa

Penguin Books Ltd, Registered Offices: 80 Strand, London WC2R ORL, England

www.penguin.com

First published 2011
1

Copyright © Jackie Holmes and Toni Maguire, 2011
All rights reserved

The moral right of the authors has been asserted

Set in 12.5/14.75pt Garamond MT Std
Typeset by Jouve (UK), Milton Keynes
Printed in England by Clays Ltd, St Ives plc

ISBN: 978-0-241-95174-3

www.greenpenguin.co.uk

Can't Anyone Help Me?

When I wrote my own story, Don't Tell Mummy, *I thought there couldn't be one that was worse. Sadly, I was wrong. Since I wrote it, I have had many letters and emails telling me of distressing, damaged childhoods. Three of them I turned into books.*

But nothing had prepared me for Jackie's story. When I received her email telling me the bare facts of her past, I was more than just upset. Horrified, moved — there are no adequate words to describe what I felt.

Phone calls followed and several emails, and a few months after the initial correspondence, Penguin agreed to publish her story. I caught a train to the north of England to meet her.

She was waiting for me at the station, a small, pretty woman with bright blue eyes who beamed at me as she introduced herself. I felt like hugging her. To have gone through what she had and be able to give me such a warm, welcoming smile — I was simply amazed.

That evening, armed with notebook and pen, I sat down with her to fill in the blanks that her email had not covered. It was I, not Jackie, who needed to take breaks as I listened to her story.

We spent two days together. At the end, I'd filled two notebooks, my arm ached, and I felt drained and relieved: drained from hearing more graphic descriptions of horror than I have ever written about before, and relieved that Jackie had been able to overcome the trauma of such a terrible childhood. And, above all, I admired the strength she had found to do so.

I believe that stories like this one have to be told, so that no abused person will ever feel that it only happened to them. Until children feel free to talk, and free of shame for the actions that are not of their making, child abuse will never be eradicated from our society.

So, thank you, Jackie, for being brave enough to tell me your story. You are truly remarkable and I hope I have done it justice.

Toni Maguire

I

An image has haunted me for thirty years. It comes to me when I am only half awake and have no control over my thoughts. But it also surfaces when I am eating, watching television, or drifting off into what I hope will be a dreamless sleep.

It is of a room where a small naked child is standing. She is so still and quiet, that little girl, so dazed. I know she is trying to think of something, anything, that will take her away from the bleak space where she is trapped. Outside the sun is shining, its warmth penetrating the brick walls of that room, but still she is shivering. She wraps her arms around her small body, raises her bony shoulders so they are almost touching her ears as she waits for what she knows is to come. For a few moments all she can hear is the pounding of her heart. Then the silence is broken by the sound she has grown to hate.

Click-click, it goes, followed by a flash that illuminates the room, exposing its bare walls and ugly metal chairs.

The little girl squeezes her eyes shut against the sudden glare.

'Open your eyes, Jackie. Open them wide for Uncle,' says the voice she recognizes. Knowing what she will see, the child unwillingly obeys and finds she is looking into the cold, blank eye of the camera's lens.

Over the years that spanned the time I have always

called 'when everything that happened, happened', she has called out to me, asking for help – but, in denial of what I see, I have always tried to push aside her desperate need.

There are other pictures and memories that try to follow, but when the first comes I stop them in their tracks.

Except when I'm unable to.

There must, I think, have been times when I was a happy child. One who chortled with glee when her father swung her in the air; scraped out a mixing bowl; ate a cake still warm from the oven; made an innocent wish when she'd blown out the candles on a birthday cake; built sandcastles on the beach; hung up a stocking for Santa; helped put up decorations at Christmas and squealed with childish joy on opening a brightly wrapped present. My mother told me there were times like that, but I cannot remember them.

I visit friends with small children, hear the sounds that are the essence of a happy home: children's spontaneous laughter, voices calling out to one another, morning sounds of teeth being scrubbed behind the bathroom door, and favourite songs sung softly along with the radio. Then I wonder if, once, my home had been like that too.

I watch curiously the joy on a toddler's face when he or she takes their first steps, and the trust of a child who has fallen, raising their arms to be picked up and kissed better by a loving parent. I see the special smiles that mothers bestow on their children who, having known nothing but love, smile radiantly back. Was I ever a child like that? Somehow, I don't think I was.

*

I want to think that as a baby my world was a warm, safe place where, lulled by my mother's voice during the day, I felt loved and secure. And at night, when I slipped into sleep, it was perhaps to the silvery notes of the mobile that hung over my cot. There is something in me that needs to imagine that my sleep was dreamless, content. I hope that my mother cuddled me as she cooed into my little pink ears before placing me in the cot. But however hard I try to conjure that image, it evades me for, of course, I cannot remember as far back as that.

Often I try to peer through the tiny peephole in time to the years before I was five, when the bad things started, for a flash of my innocent past. Sometimes a memory I haven't managed to suppress emerges and what I see makes a little sense. At other times it is too painful for me to give it more than a hasty glance before, cowardly, I push it away.

At night, dreams of hazy images or of darkness, with a feeling of being out of control, drift into my subconscious and force me awake. Those frighten me but there is one that is worse than all the others: the one that has come time after time for as long as I can remember; the one whose tendrils cling to me even after I have woken.

In that dream, there is a small child. I cannot see her tiny figure, only feel her presence. She is in a windowless room where she knows there is a door, but she cannot see it for the darkness has blinded her. Round and round she runs, her hands outstretched as, scrabbling at the walls, her fingers search desperately for a smooth surface or a crack where that door must be. She knows that if she fails to find it, something terrible will happen.

7

In my sleep, her panic and terror transmit themselves to me and I feel what she feels. I sense that someone else is there, someone intent on destroying her. Terrified, I open my mouth to scream. It is then that cold hands cover my mouth, smothering the sound. There is a weight pressing against my throat and I cannot breathe. Choking, I writhe with the effort of gasping for air. I hear a voice calling my name – and then I'm back in my brightly lit bedroom: in my house the lights always remain on. But still I clutch at my bedding as my mouth fills with that thick sour taste: the terrible taste of my childhood.

My eyes dart around the familiar surroundings and, for a few seconds, I fear that the creature that lived in my nightmare has followed me. But the bedside light illuminates every corner of the room and I see that it is empty – but even then I am not reassured.

2

There are times when, in the small hours of the morning, the recurring dream wakes me and I fight sleep, fearing its return. It is then that those snippets of my past force their way into my thoughts, tormenting me as they make me feel, again and again, the pain that I lived with for such a long time. And as I lie still, my hands curled around the edges of my pillow, I search my mind for the child who was once me. That little girl who, when she came into the world, had no knowledge of the horrors that awaited her. I want to ask her one question, then tell her she must leave me for ever. But, however hard I try, I cannot find her.

It is when the fear and anxiety that the dream has left in its wake makes my heart beat faster and my hands dampen that I climb out of bed. I go to the cupboard where the proof that she lived exists on sheets of paper. Not written in a padlocked diary, which spans the time between childhood and teenage years, by a happy child, but by the psychologists and psychiatrists of Social Services on their formal stationery. Their reports gave their opinions, their diagnoses and their comments. All these assessments were collated and placed in an official-looking lever arch file, which was finally handed to my adult self. I take it down and start turning the pages.

The first report I read documents an interview between a psychologist to whom my school had referred me and my parents. In it, the psychologist wrote less about the child whose problems he had been asked to analyse than he did about the details my parents had given him. He stated that my mother had informed him that when I was little more than a toddler I had started to change into a difficult child. One who had become nervous and fretful, who woke with a start and cried at the slightest sudden sound. No questions were asked as to whether anything had changed in that little girl's life or if my parents could remember something that might have triggered the stress.

But by the time that first psychologist had seen the child he had written about so sparingly, the damage had already taken root. Rage, one of the strongest of all emotions, had already started to grow deep within her. Just a tiny drop to begin with, sometimes disguised by the occasional smile and her childish chatter as she learnt to form words and sentences. It went unnoticed but, still, it was there.

But emotions have no need for words: they are stored as unlabelled facts in the recesses of our minds. And the anger the small child felt, an anger well documented in that file, was directed at her primary carer: her mother. If she was left alone in a room, her frustrated screams filled the house. When she was given food, she threw it on the floor. She would only sleep if a night light was left burning. And as she grew, so did her rage, until one day it erupted.

When I was first given the file I asked myself the same questions my parents had asked of the many specialists I was taken to. At what age do the self-destructive emotions of rage, bewilderment and fear infiltrate the mind to create a disturbed child? Yes, they asked that, but they didn't ask why they occurred.

The correct answer, I know now, was 'At the moment the adult world betrays the child, shattering their sense of safety.' But that reply was never forthcoming. I wondered what the specialist had said to them instead. Whatever it was, no written notes recorded it.

Instead, over the next few years the psychologists documented the times I had throat infections, without any thought as to what might have caused them, and wrote pages of praise for my parents at their forbearance in dealing with their problem child.

The specialists I was taken to wrote page after page, in their impersonal clinical language, of my descent from troubled three-year-old to disturbed teenager. But, like my parents, never once did one of those specialists ask the critical question: why? Why did a child from such a supposedly good home background display all the symptoms that she did? The facts were in front of them, but instead of asking what was wrong with my life they asked another question: what was wrong with me? Then, unable to think that any outside influence could have been the cause, they gave me coloured plastic bricks to build with and puzzles to work out, as though how I completed them would show the level of my intelligence and the deep inner workings of my mind.

It is when I get to the section of the file where the reports document how my behaviour became the talk of our village, and my parents accused me of bringing shame to our family, that the words blur, making it impossible for me to read any further.

It is always when I come to those pages that I put the file down, for that part I can remember only too well. Reading those impersonal words still has the power to bring back the humiliation and rage that I was made to feel then. Instead I open a small manila packet, the one containing the photographs of my family and myself. One by one I take them out and study each picture, as I have done so many times before.

There is a child dressed in shorts and a T-shirt, whose flaxen hair is tied back in a thick plait. Another shows her in a dark blue velvet dress when she was a bridesmaid at a winter wedding, surrounded by happy faces. There she is again, aged around seven, smiling almost tentatively up at her father. There is even one of her as a teenager, caught unaware, talking to her mother while they sit in the garden. Of course I know the girl is me, but I cannot remember one of the occasions on which those photos were taken.

I search each picture for the child I once was. But, however hard I look, these images are of a stranger. I can see her pain and her fragility – but I do not know her.

There is one more photo, its face turned down. My hand hovers over it. The urge to pick it up is as inexplicable as the urge to scrape a partly healed scab with a sharp fingernail, then watch it ooze blood. It is the one picture that has the power to transport me back in time.

In a pink cotton dress and surrounded by soft toys, a small child gazes unwaveringly into the camera. She looks neither shy, as so many children do when a camera is aimed at them, nor animated as she stares unblinkingly into the lens.

But why would she? She was no stranger to a camera. Photo after photo had already been taken of her but, of course, none of those others had ever been pasted into the family album. By the time this picture was taken the child had not just suffered horrific abuse but had learnt about rejection and betrayal by those who should have protected her.

It is then that the image that haunts me in my dreams is in front of my eyes again, this time clear, painfully in focus, and I am unable to push it away.

'There's a good girl,' she hears that voice say to her again. The voice she recognizes. She tries to see where it's coming from – she knows he is somewhere behind the tripod and the white light – but all she can see is a dark shadow where he must be.

Click-click, the camera goes again.

'Smile for me, Jackie,' says the disembodied voice. 'Lower your hands, turn around – there, that's better, that's what I want.' Each time she does exactly as he asks.

At last it is over and her uncle comes over to where she is standing, a man who is always immaculate. His thick dark-blond hair is brushed smoothly back from a surprisingly youthful face. He's somewhere in his forties, but only a hint of his age shows behind the deep tan that comes from the sun and the tanning booths.

The little girl looks into the face she knows so well, watches his mouth with the plump lower lip, a mouth that seems too small for the face, with its sharp planes and piercing blue eyes, forming the words that only he ever says to her. 'Such a good girl you are – such a pretty little one too. There, that didn't hurt you, did it?' Sweets, a

13

child's reward for good behaviour, are pressed into her hand. Warm hands caress her, smooth back her hair, then help her into her clothes. 'I love you,' he says then. 'I love you as though you are my own daughter. When you're not here, I look at your pictures. They're all I have until you come back.

'Come to me,' he says, and as he opens his arms, she walks into them.

'So special,' he murmurs, as his arms wrap around her small body. 'So innocent, so precious.' And she, feeling safe again, leans against him, her small form appearing almost boneless as she rests against his much larger one.

3

It is when I see that image that the others refuse to stay away. It is as though a projector held by malevolent hands is flicking them over faster and faster. Then I am forced to remember those other times, the times when he played what he called 'the game'.

'The game' always started with him blindfolding her. When she first played it, it seemed innocent and it was one that the little girl liked. She trusted the man and wondered what surprises would come her way this time. Childish giggles would escape her when the soft strip of material was tied over her eyes. 'Open your mouth,' he would say, and obediently she would do so.

First, a small piece of chocolate was placed between her lips. 'What's that? Tell me and you can have another piece.'

'Chocolate,' she would say enthusiastically, then smile with anticipation at the thought of another piece, which, dutifully, he gave her.

Next a small soft toy animal was pressed into her hands. 'If you get this right, you can keep it,' her uncle would tell her, as her small fingers stroked the fur in her search for ears or tail that would give her a clue as to which animal it was.

As her vocabulary grew and she became more adroit at naming them, her collection of soft toys expanded – a cat, a pink rabbit and a red elephant soon belonged to her, as did some more unusual species. A green and brown felt tortoise, a spotted long-necked giraffe, which she had needed help in naming, and an Australian bush baby, which she had thought was a big-eyed teddy bear.

It was after they had played the game for a while that something else was placed in her mouth. Something that filled it, making her cheeks bulge and her throat tighten in protest. Her body jerked, her hands flew to her mouth, but one of her uncle's much larger hands covered hers as he whispered soothing words before he removed the thing.

The next time they played the game, she eyed him warily but only nice-tasting things were placed in her mouth and another soft toy was added to her collection. The last thing he spooned into her mouth was thick ice-cream and, despite the blindfold, she could sense him watching her enjoyment.

It was not until the game had continued for several weeks that it was spoilt for her for ever. It started off as usual, with small pieces of chocolate, but no sooner had she swallowed the last than that thing was in her mouth again. She tried to wriggle away but this time he held her head so she couldn't move.

'Good girl,' he said, over and over, but then his voice changed, grew thicker until she hardly recognized it as his. She heard another noise, almost like the one her mother's dog had made when it had hurt its paw – a whimpering sound followed by a groan. Her hands rose in protest and tried to push his away. The hands that were holding her head shook, and then her mouth filled with something that

16

tasted sour and horrid. It trickled down her throat making her gag. He released her but she choked and retched until there was nothing left. The bitter taste lingered.

He took the blindfold off, but this time he avoided looking directly at her, as though he couldn't bear to see the reproach that shone out of her tear-filled eyes.

He brought her some ice-cream – 'Come, Jackie, there's nothing to be frightened of, that's all it was.' She didn't believe him and turned away, her back stiff with indignation at his actions.

But when she heard his voice telling her how much she was loved and that she was just being silly, she allowed him to place her on his knee. Gradually, as the soothing words were whispered over and over, she relaxed and her head fell on to his shoulder.

It was he who bathed her after those games. 'Must get you nice and clean before your auntie comes back from work,' he would say. Then, taking her hand, he would lead her up the stairs to the bathroom where sweet-smelling liquid was poured under the tap. She was placed in the warm water and the foam came up to her chin. A little yellow duck floated in the bubbles, a sponge trickled water down her back, and when he lifted her out and gently dried every crevice of her body, she said no more of what had happened in that room.

Those are two of the memories I have of the time before I started school; another lurks constantly in my subconscious, one so painful that I want to leave it there unexamined, but so often I cannot.

4

I grew up in a pretty Yorkshire village where new estates of large, detached houses had mushroomed on the outskirts and many of its small terrace houses had been transformed into second homes for wealthy city people. Hedges were neatly clipped; front gardens were immaculate. The three pubs were adorned year round with flower-filled hanging baskets, and the pretty exteriors of the shops were repainted annually in vibrant colours, yellow, turquoise and plum.

It was a place where supermarkets were only allowed to open if they were totally out of sight of the village, fish-and-chip shops were banned and the council had never been able to get permission to build the small grey boxlike houses that were badly needed for the lower-income population.

The local school was considered one of the best in the area – after all, no riff-raff was allowed in to corrupt the children of the well-to do. Crime was minimal so front doors and garden sheds were seldom locked.

To anyone who did not know the truth, I was a lucky child. I lived in a lovely house. My parents were well off and, to the outsider, appeared to be caring and supportive.

I had a brother, but in a way I never knew him. He was in his mid-teens when I was born and already away at university by the time I started school. He arrived home for Christmas and his summer holidays when I was small, but his visits dwindled as he made new friends. Or maybe I had driven him away. I knew my mother thought so. I had heard her say it to my father.

Whatever the reason, by the time I was old enough to file memories away, there was a barrier between my mother and me that was never breached. Maybe she was embarrassed that just when her contemporaries were rinsing the grey out of their hair and enrolling for yoga classes she had to announce that a baby was on the way. One that I learnt at an early age was definitely a mistake.

Certainly the estate where we lived seemed bereft of small children, and my mother's friends, with teenagers already studying away from home, could not provide me with company of a suitable age. I was therefore totally dependent on the adult world.

Friends called, and I, in a crisp cotton frock if it was summer or a woollen pinafore dress and jumper if it was cold, sat tongue-tied throughout the visit and listened to their chatter. Playing outside and getting dirty was not on my mother's agenda so, bored and apparently invisible, I would sit without moving until they were so engrossed in their adult conversation that I could slip away unobserved.

My parents, like their nearby neighbours, lived in a fake stone four-bedroomed detached house with a double garage and a beautifully maintained garden. With her eye for decorative detail my mother had supervised the several makeovers the house had had since they had first moved in. By the time I was old enough to appreciate or even notice the décor, a wooden bar with an array of bottles, optics firmly in place, had been built at one end of the long sitting room. Settees covered with a light-coloured subtly patterned fabric, their thick cushions plumped constantly, flanked a large stone fireplace, and against the wall opposite them, a blond oak cabinet housed the television and music centre. The dining room was furnished with more blond wood. The kitchen, with its padded built-in seating and pine table, was decorated with cheerful shades of yellow and trimmed with sparkling white. The floor, where there was never a stain, was one large seamless strip of the same bright shades.

My mother was proud of the house – 'Tidiness is next to godliness' was one of her much-repeated sayings, not that she was a frequent churchgoer. From as far back as I can remember, I knew never to leave anything out of place. When visitors arrived, they always found something new to admire – a painting or an elaborate flower arrangement. But beneath their words, a hint of envy often showed.

'Oh, Dora, how beautiful! You have such good taste,' or 'Aren't you clever!' they said, when they were shown my mother's latest acquisition. Her face would light up with pleasure.

The only thing that an observant guest might have wondered was why every bedroom in the house, including mine, was dominated by a very large double bed. In our area it was usual for there to be one twin-bedded room in case an unmarried couple or two friends came to stay. But not in my parents' house. I never questioned it while I was young, and by the time I was old enough to notice, I had already learnt the reason why.

But even then I was aware that respectability, or the

face of it, was important to my parents, and certainly no one who came into contact with them could have thought they were anything but the epitome of it.

My mother, with her discreetly highlighted hair, scorned anything that could be labelled 'common', which included the synthetic fabrics for jackets and dresses that were popular during the seventies. Instead, she favoured the natural fibres, such as cotton, linen and wool, that the designers of Jaeger, Max Mara and, for very special occasions, Jean Muir used in their understated clothes. Pearls were worn by day, a single strand around her neck and small studs in her ears, and she never left the house without her hair in place and her makeup on. Appearances mattered – not just to her but to my father as well. He wore the uniforms of the successful businessman and the devoted family man he wanted the world to see: dark pin-striped suits with white shirts and discreet ties from Monday to Friday, cords and tweed jackets at weekends.

I thought my parents' bedroom was the most beautiful room in the house: pale peach walls and cream curtains without a hint of the masculinity my father might have preferred. A thick silk bedspread in a deeper tone lay on the massive bed, with its piles of carefully positioned pillows. An archway led into their en-suite bathroom, with its large deep white bath and gold taps.

It was a room in which my mother enjoyed spending time alone. She smoothed lotions on to her limbs, restorative creams on her face and neck and took long, leisurely, fragrant baths. I liked to stand there when she was getting ready for a night out or just for the day, inhaling the different perfumes from the many jars that stood around the bath. Not that I ever had a chance to stand there for long: when she saw me hovering, a look of irritation would cross her face. 'What do you want now, Jackie?' she would ask. When I was small, fearing her displeasure, I was unable to answer her question. I could not put into words what I wanted, but I longed to hear from her the same words that were uttered by my uncle. I never did.

Instead of putting loving arms around me and saying caring words, she would dismiss me: 'Well, if you don't want anything, go and find something to do and let me get on with what I'm doing,' was one of her abrupt reprimands. If I waited too long to retreat, a well-shaped eyebrow was raised and another regularly used sentence would follow: 'For heaven's sake, Jackie! I don't know why you're always under my feet when you have everything you could possibly want in your own room.' She would say this whether she was seated or not, which confused me. How could I be under her feet if she was in the bath or sitting on the bed?

'Now, you're old enough to amuse yourself for a few minutes, aren't you?' I knew my presence was unwelcome and would walk desolately away to my gold and cream room with its adult furniture.

In there my friends lived. They consisted of the teddy bears and other stuffed animals that had been given to me as presents. There were some that I was told not to play with: they were what my mother called 'collector's items'. An antique bear from a manufacturer called Steiff sat out of reach on a high shelf. It was to be admired, she said, but not hugged, and next to it was a beautiful mohair bear with 'Merrythought' on his left paw. The latest addition to my collection was Paddington, who wore a brown felt hat and a red duffel coat and shiny blue wellington boots. Like the others, his bright eyes watched my every move. And there was the friend whom nobody but I knew about: Florence, the little girl who had the qualities of her *Magic Roundabout* namesake – kindness and patience. Only there, in the privacy of my room, could she step out of my imagination, join the bears and keep me company. It was to that little group I talked when I sat them in a circle around me and took out the dolls' tea set. I told them about my mother's bad temper but I didn't tell them about my uncle playing 'the game'. That was a secret, to be kept locked at the back of my mind; a secret that already had started to torment me even when I slept.

5

I do not know when I learnt the word that described my parents' weekend activities. I just understood, during those very early years, that they loved entertaining and being entertained. It seemed to me then that every weekend was taken up with preparing for guests or spending time getting ready to visit them. Not wanting a small child in the house and often needing my bedroom for overnight guests, my parents sent me several miles away to the village where my aunt and uncle, who were also my godparents, lived.

'Not quite in the same class as ours,' I heard my mother say condescendingly, on more than one occasion, about the area where her brother lived. And when I became old enough to notice the difference, I saw that she was right.

My aunt and uncle lived in an ugly red-brick semi, surrounded by others that looked just the same. Only the gardens lent any individuality to the estate. Some had small square lawns, others were a riot of colour nearly all year round, and a few were whimsical, with plaster gnomes wearing idiotic grins and holding miniature fishing rods on the edge of tiny ponds. In one or two children's toys were left carelessly out, and a battered family saloon with a 'baby on board' sign in the back window was parked on a patch of worn grass.

My aunt and uncle's house, with two round bushes standing in terracotta urns at either side of the front door, was definitely of the small-green-lawn type. Without the benefit of bay windows, which several of their neighbours had installed, it had an entirely flat façade with white UPVC window-frames and door. Like most of his neighbours, my uncle had to park on the street, for the garage had been turned into an office for him to work from.

Every weekend when my uncle collected me, he stopped at a florist's to buy roses for his wife – scentless, thornless, brightly coloured buds that had been grown in heated greenhouses, quite unlike the lush scented ones that came from our garden. When we reached the house, the ones he had bought the week before had begun to droop and shed their petals. They were taken out of the vase and placed in the bin outside the back door. Rustling cellophane was removed from the new bunch, and those he arranged carefully in clean water, then placed the vase back on the sideboard.

As soon as my aunt returned from work her eyes would dart in the direction of the flowers. On seeing the expected new arrangement, she would utter the same phrase as she did every week – 'For me?' – as though someone else might be the recipient of his generosity.

'You sit down, dear, take the weight off your feet,' he would say, as he did every time. On would go the kettle as, with a grateful smile, she settled her ample self on a chair, kicking off her sensible flat leather shoes that were, by this time, pinching her swollen feet.

'He's so good to me,' she would tell everyone, whenever she had the opportunity. 'Can't do enough for me.' Her round face, under its cap of neatly cut mousy brown hair, would glow as she recounted his many kindnesses and her luck at having married such a considerate man.

Unlike my parents' home, where my mother's income – from the antiques shop my father had bought for her to oversee – was used for luxuries, my aunt and uncle needed all they earned to live on. I knew that because it was repeatedly mentioned to me.

My uncle worked in the week at something I was never really clear about, while my aunt worked part-time in a shop; she was always needed on their busiest day – Saturday. That was the one day I was always left entirely in his care.

There were only a few weekends when I could not go there on a Saturday, other than when my aunt and uncle took their annual holiday. If my mother heard my uncle or aunt sneeze or they sounded thick with a cold on the telephone, she would announce with a sigh that I must remain at home.

'Before everything happened' I would wail with disappointment for I was bored and lonely with either playing on my own in the garden or in my room.

My mother's routine over those rare weekends when I was at home left her little time to notice me. 'You've got plenty of toys to play with,' she would say, when I complained that I had nothing to do. And in a way she was right: in my room I had everything that a small child could have wished for – dolls, toys and a wardrobe full of the latest fashions in expensive children's clothing. But what I really wanted was someone to play with, another child to talk to, or even some attention from my parents. But none of that was forthcoming.

On Saturday mornings my father always played golf. Despite my mother's protests that she needed someone to keep an eye on me, he would refuse to cancel his game just because I was going to be at home for the weekend.

'Oh, well, Jackie,' she would say, with a sigh that told me how inconvenient it was to have me there, 'you'll have to come with me. Just mind you're good.' I would be armed with a colouring book and a box of wax crayons, and she would drive us into the village centre.

Her routine seldom varied on Saturday morning. First it was the hairdresser, and I would sit in the waiting area swinging my legs as I watched her hair being washed and blow-dried. Her long nails were professionally filed, buffed and painted, and she would flap her hands in the air to dry the varnish. She flicked through magazines and drank coffee, while I was given orange juice and a children's book I couldn't read.

On the days that she was entertaining, last-minute shopping had to be done. We would visit the butcher and the greengrocer where she would have an animated conversation about the quality of each item she wanted before she bought anything. Then it was back to the house where, after a hasty lunch of something healthy, such as a small salad and fruit, I was told to stay out of the way and amuse myself in the garden. 'Don't get dirty,' she would warn, as I went outside.

It was on one of those weekends that I learnt a little more about my parents' weekend interests. I had seen that the beautifully set table's extra leaves were in use so that it could seat eight people. My mother had covered it with a lace cloth and her best silver cutlery, crystal wine glasses and china. Linen napkins were folded on each side plate and she had arranged flowers in the centre, with tall candles in elaborate antique candlesticks. As I wandered from the garden to the kitchen, I smelt the delicious aromas of the food she was cooking.

'Who's coming?' I asked, even though I knew I would be told very firmly to stay in my room and not leave it.

'Oh, just some friends, no one you really know,' my mother replied, in a more friendly voice than usual. 'I'll feed you first, and as a treat you can watch a video upstairs in your room.' When she noticed my apparent lack of interest, the friendly tone was replaced with the more familiar impatient one. 'Jackie,' she said sharply, 'very few people have video recorders in their houses, and there you are with one in your own room. At least look grateful.'

I mumbled my thanks but inside I felt growing resentment: I understood only too well that a film was just her way of getting rid of me.

I had my supper in the kitchen, then was sent upstairs, where my father had found a suitable film that he had already placed in the video recorder for me to watch. It was later, long after the film had finished and my mother had come upstairs to put me to bed, that I tossed and turned as sleep eluded me.

I could hear music playing softly, and after the doorbell chimed, my mother greeting new arrivals. The sounds of laughter and chatter drifted up from the sitting room, and eventually I dozed off.

Later, when it was dark outside, I woke up. For a few moments I felt disoriented, but realized gradually that noise from downstairs had woken me. Curious – our house was not one in which loud laughter rang out often – I crept out of bed and down the stairs.

At first the group of adults in the sitting room did not notice me standing in the doorway, watching the strangers that my parents had turned into. My mother, her face flushed, a drink in her hand, was sitting on one of the settees. Her skirt had ridden up above her knees, showing far more leg than I had ever seen her display before, and instead of my father, one of her friends' husbands was sitting next to her. My eyes opened wide when I saw his arm around her shoulders and his hand stroking her neck. As I watched, his fingers trailed down until they slid under the fabric of her lacy top.

I glanced around the room for my father and saw him leaning back on one of our easy chairs with the other man's wife jigging around on his knee. His hand was under her skirt, her blonde head was against his chest and her fingers were stroking his hair. The other two couples were dancing slowly to the music but I had seen them often enough to know that they had changed partners. I felt a twinge of unease. I was witnessing something that I was too small to understand but that glimpse of adult life unsettled me. I already wished I hadn't seen it. I just wanted to go back to my room and climb under the bedclothes before I was seen. But somehow I was unable to move.

It was my mother's friend who saw me first. Her head rose and she squealed, then tried to remove herself hastily from my father's lap. 'Dora,' she called to my mother, 'we have a little visitor.'

My mother opened her eyes, lifted her head and looked angrily in my direction. Her face went even redder as she jumped away from her friend's husband, brushing his hand off her. She marched to where I was, grabbed my arm and pulled me up the stairs. 'Just stay in your bed like I told you,' she snapped.

I had broken her rule that I should never come downstairs after I had been put to bed, so I said nothing, just curled into a ball and tried to go back to sleep. But no matter how hard I tried, my brain was working furiously, trying to make sense of what I had seen, which it failed to do successfully. Throughout the night I heard more bursts of laughter, footsteps on the stairs and my mother's voice sounding different from her usual well-modulated tones: it was higher-pitched and slightly slurred. A man's voice that I knew was not my father's spoke to her. Then doors opened and closed and the sounds became muffled.

Again, I was driven by curiosity to find out what was happening, and even though I knew I'd be in trouble if I was caught, I crept out of my room and along the corridor to where the other three bedrooms were. My parents' door was shut, as was the second bedroom's, but the third was ajar. Unable to resist temptation, I placed my eye to the crack and saw my father with a woman, the one he had been with downstairs. This time she was kneeling on the bed, naked. Her face was turned away from me, but I recognized her long blonde hair, which now hung around her shoulders. My father, also undressed, was kneeling behind her. His hands held her hips and he was moving back and forwards. As I watched, his movements became faster until his body jerked and his shout mixed with the woman's high-pitched yelps.

I felt sick and wished, as I had earlier, that I had obeyed

my mother and stayed in my room. I might not have understood then what I had witnessed but it added to my earlier unease. I crept away from the door as quietly as I could – I knew that the two people inside the room would be very angry if they saw me.

Nothing was said to me the next day about what I had witnessed the night before. My mother was her usual brisk, efficient self as she bustled around the kitchen, shooing me out of the way as she prepared the Sunday lunch, and my father hardly raised his head from the pile of newspapers.

But the next weekend my uncle arrived. 'Coming to stay with us, darling,' he said, ruffling my hair.

'I hope she's not too much trouble,' my mother said, as she always did, in a voice that conveyed she was not interested either way.

He flashed her a white-toothed smile and gave the expected answer. 'Oh, she's such a good little thing. Aren't you, sugar?' With those words, his smile included me in its warmth. 'You mustn't worry, Dora, we love having her to stay. She's no trouble at all.' Then he picked up my small case, with a change of clothes, my pyjamas and my special Paddington Bear, and led me to his car.

On the drive to his house he drove with one hand on the wheel, the other touching my hand or stroking my legs. 'Is anything the matter?' he asked, for images of the weekend before had temporarily rendered me silent. I shook my head.

'You know you can tell me anything, don't you?' he continued. I nodded.

'You're my special little girl, aren't you?'

Hearing his words, I felt the knot of unease start to uncoil in my stomach.

It was just a week before I was due to start school. I was holding Paddington tightly that day. Summer was ending, the sun was thinner and the leaves had already started dropping from the trees. I can still picture myself checking that Paddington's duffel coat was buttoned up tightly to keep him warm.

But what I remember most about that day is my uncle taking me to meet his friend.

6

'You'll like it there,' he had told me. 'There will be other children for you to play with.' I felt pleased then; it was so rare that I was able to be with children of my own age. Children were not little people to my mother: they were nuisances who might trample dirt into the house, make a noise, or leave their toys scattered on the furniture. Friends who already had small grandchildren visited us periodically when they were babysitting. They handed the infants over to me to entertain either in the garden or in the furthest part of the sitting room, where an eye could be kept on me and my small charges.

'Jackie's so good with the little ones,' a bright voice would say.

Looking down at a gurgling toddler, I would wish it was a child of my own age, whom I could talk to and play more interesting games with.

My uncle kept up a light patter of conversation with me as we drove to the outskirts of the town. Instead of turning towards where he and my aunt lived, he drove straight on towards the old run-down area, with its warren of narrow streets and rows of terraced houses.

He pulled up outside one that looked even less cared-for than the rest. Although it was still daylight, the curtains were closed, giving it a shuttered, deserted look. Weeds grew between the cracks of the broken paving stones that made a short path, while the small front garden had scarcely a tuft of grass, far less a flower or shrub. The porch we stood under when we rang the bell was just a cap of concrete roofing, designed to protect anyone standing there from the rain. But that day it was sunny, and I remember looking over my shoulder as a gust of wind blew an empty plastic bag along the deserted street. It whirled up high, and I watched as it disappeared from sight.

The door we were facing had, some years earlier, been a dark green, but the paint had worn off in patches, and long splinters of wood were missing from the bottom edge. I wondered who lived there, for it was not the sort of place I had ever visited before.

A thin, slightly stooped man, whose head, apart from a fringe of white hair, was almost bald, opened the door to us. His pale grey eyes blinked from the bright light that the door let in, and then he smiled a welcome. Without uttering a word he gestured for us to enter the tiny hall. As we stepped inside my uncle placed his hand on my back and gently pushed me into what he said was the sitting room.

It was a shabby, dimly lit room that smelt of stale smoke, beer and neglect. Worn furniture stood on lino that attempted to look like pine floorboards. A coffee-table, stained with the white rings made by countless wet bottles and hot mugs, stood in the centre of the room, but the focal point was the large television. It was clear that the man spent much of his time watching it, for all the furniture was oriented in its direction. The sound was turned right down but there were flickering images on the screen, and I noticed that the man had left his glasses on the arm of the two-seater settee.

'Been watching movies,' he said to my uncle, with a snigger, as though that explained why the curtains were drawn in the middle of the day. The two men exchanged a look that managed to be both secretive and knowing; a look that, in its exclusion of me, sent prickles of unease through me. I wanted to leave the room, go back outside, get into the car and for my uncle to drive us away but, unable to express those feelings, I just stood there without speaking.

A boy, a few years older than me with a mop of dark chestnut hair curling around his ears, came into the room. Dressed in jeans and an un-ironed grey T-shirt, he was, like the room, unkempt and neglected.

'Ah, Dave,' the man said, 'take this pretty little girl into the garden, will you, and give her some lemonade?' Now I saw the man and the boy exchange a look that I didn't understand.

The boy took my hand and led me out of the room into the kitchen, where he picked up a bottle of what he told me was lemonade. He then took me outside and, as he passed me the bottle, I noticed a rim of dirt under the chewed-down edges of his fingernails.

The nervousness I had felt ever since I had gone into the house had made my throat dry and I gulped the drink, hardly tasting it. At the bottom of the garden, a gate led to a path with a river flowing alongside it. The boy beckoned to me to follow him. He said nothing, just started gathering up smooth stones. I began to help him. Once there was a small pile, he threw them one by one across the water with a quick twist of his wrist. I stood beside him, watching the ripples they made as they skimmed across the surface.

'Let me try too,' I said.

He smiled at me. 'Your hands are too small,' he said, but he gave me one of the smaller stones.

He was right, my wrists were not strong enough to spin it, and the stone dropped straight into the water and sank.

I can't remember any more than that, whether we played any games or what we talked about, only what happened in the house when we went back inside.

'Got something for you two to watch,' the man said, motioning for us to sit on the settee.

The boy and I sat as we were told to do, side by side. His hand crept across the space between us and held mine. Did he feel sorry for me because he knew what was to happen next? Or was it for his own comfort that he held the hand of a child who hadn't even turned six?

I was handed some more lemonade.

'Drink it all up, Jackie,' my uncle said, when I tried to put the glass on the floor. I felt the other man's eyes watching me, and the combined pressure of his gaze and my uncle's words made me swallow it. It was sweet, far sweeter than any drink I had been given before, and I started to feel sleepy.

The film began, and suddenly I was looking at a naked woman on all fours with a man positioned behind her, gripping her buttocks. Another man came on to the screen and, within seconds, there were three naked bodies all joined together. I pulled my hand away from the boy's and tried to look away. I didn't want to see it.

'It's what people do, Jackie,' said my uncle, and underneath the warmth of his voice there was a sudden firmness. 'I want you to watch it.'

He hadn't told me anything I didn't already know – I had glimpsed as much through that bedroom door – but still I kept my head turned.

My uncle forced me to move up so he could sit next to me. I put my fingers over my eyes but nothing could block out the grunts and squeals coming from the television. The boy pulled my hand away from my face, then gently laced his fingers through mine. 'Do as he says and watch it,' he whispered, squeezing my fingers reassuringly. 'They'll get cross if we don't.' My uncle had never been cross with me before so I wasn't afraid. I just wanted him to take me away from there, out of that grubby room, which suddenly felt very hot. On the TV I could see groups of naked people, their bodies contorted into various positions and their faces shiny with sweat, performing acts that disgusted me.

Out of the corner of my eye I saw my uncle leaving the room and, panic-stricken that I was alone with the man and the boy, I tried to run after him.

It was the man who stopped me. His hard fingers gripped my shoulders. 'Stay here, girl,' he said. 'Your uncle's just gone to the car. He'll be back in a tick.' Frightened now, I sat down on the settee again.

Within a few minutes my uncle returned, only this time he was carrying something: his camera equipment. I wondered, as he set up his tripod, what he was going to photograph.

'Come, Jackie,' he said, 'get undressed.'

My body quivered with the fear of something unknown

and the shame of being asked to undress in front of two complete strangers. I tried to shake my head. But as I moved it, I felt faint and the room swam around me.

'Jackie, have some more lemonade – it'll make you feel better,' the boy said. Another glass full of the light-coloured liquid appeared. I took it and put it to my mouth as I looked pleadingly over the rim at my uncle. He wouldn't really make me take my clothes off in front of these strangers, would he?

Faintness overcame me and I crumpled to the floor. I felt my uncle's hands on me as he roughly pulled off my clothes until I was naked, apart from my shoes and socks.

'Now, Jackie,' he said, 'I'm making a film and you are a little actress. All you have to do is the same things as those people were doing on the television. Do you understand me?' His voice sounded as though he was a long way away, but when I looked, he was standing close to the boy who had already taken off his jeans and T-shirt.

He was thin. I could see the outline of his ribs rising and falling as he breathed. Apart from the deep purple of bruises on his arms and back, his skin was pale, as though it was seldom exposed to the sun. Standing there naked, he looked vulnerable and childish.

'Dave will show you what to do – he's an old hand at this, aren't you, son?' the man said, and I noticed a sullen, defeated look cross the boy's face as he muttered, 'Yes, Dad.' I didn't know whether he had agreed that he was an old hand or that he was going to show me what to do.

Then the boy's voice changed and a pleading note came into it. 'But, Dad, she's so young, do I have to?'

No sooner were the words out of his mouth than the man's face darkened and he raised his fist.

It was my uncle who spoke then, his words stopping the man's hand landing on the boy. 'That's enough,' he said, and the hand fell to the man's side. 'Dave's a good boy, aren't you?' my uncle added, cajoling.

Again I heard the muttered 'Yes.'

The boy leant over me. His mouth covered mine as he kissed me. I felt his tongue slide between my lips. His hands stroked my body, then slid between my legs, and all the time I could hear the man instructing his son on what to do next.

Click-click, went the camera.

'Turn round, son, get your legs behind her. Now lick her.'

The boy's legs went around my neck as he turned and pressed his mouth to the part I thought was completely private. I felt something soft and damp move between my legs and tried to squeeze them together.

'Part your legs, Jackie.' This time the words were spoken by my uncle, and when my legs did not move, it was his touch I felt drawing them wide apart.

Lights flashed as my uncle filmed the boy licking and fingering every inch of my shivering body.

Later, it was the man who lifted me and placed me in the same position that the boy had been in.

My head was held by adult hands and something hard pressed against my mouth. I wanted to move, but I was too sleepy to try.

At last it was over and I fell asleep. Voices entered my dream. I saw the man's face swimming towards me, felt something in my mouth, something I wanted to spit out but had not the energy to do so. Once again I fell asleep.

When I woke, only my uncle and I were in the room. I was fully dressed. The curtains were still closed, but the television was off and there was no camera equipment. My mouth tasted sour and felt sore, my head pounded and I wanted to be sick. My uncle handed me another drink but this time it was not so sweet. 'This will make you feel better,' he said, although I had not told him I felt ill.

'Where are they?' I mumbled.

'Why, Jackie, you've been asleep all afternoon,' my uncle told me, without answering my question. 'You've been dreaming.'

For a while, I believed him, believed that nothing had happened, and, like my nightmares, I pushed the events of that afternoon to the back of my mind. That belief lasted until he introduced me to another friend and then another.

But that first time I still felt I could trust him. I picked up Paddington, who was now sitting beside me, walked on shaking legs out to the car and climbed in.

7

The day I had been dreading was fast approaching. All week my mother had rushed me to shops to buy new clothes and shoes. 'You'll like school,' she said, with an assurance I didn't share. 'You'll make lots of little friends there.'

School. Just the word made my stomach churn.

I didn't want to be with strangers, to have to talk to them or sit with them.

Strangers frightened me now.

The week before I was due to start, my sleep was constantly disturbed by nightmares. I dreamt of trying to escape from something I had no name for, of feeling pressure in my throat and of choking. When I woke it was to tears running down my face and the taste of something thick and sour in my mouth. Once I screamed so loudly that my father came running into my room.

'What's the matter, Jackie? Another bad dream?' he asked, and put his arm around me.

I stiffened and froze – the thought of moist lips touching my cheek repelled me. I managed to whisper, 'Yes.'

He pulled the duvet gently up around me, brushed my hair away from my face and I felt him standing beside my bed, watching me. He sighed deeply before he left me huddled under the bedclothes, pretending I had already slipped back into sleep. And when I did, other dreams slid into my subconscious, dreams that made me twist and turn. When the morning sounds of the household rescued me, the remnants of those nightmares still lingered. My head felt heavy, my stomach hollow, and a sinking feeling of dread ran through me.

No matter how much I complained or how dark the shadows under my eyes from lack of sleep, nothing was going to stop my mother getting me ready that first morning.

Unceremoniously she pulled the bedclothes off me when I tried to cling to them, jerking me on to the floor. I clutched at the door jamb, wailing that I didn't want to go, but she took no notice of my distress and just prised my fingers away. 'Jackie, you're going to school whether you like it or not so stop your nonsense now,' she shouted, in exasperation. I sobbed and told her I didn't want to, but she just became angrier.

My new clothes were pulled over my head, my hair was brushed roughly and plaited, a ribbon tied to the end, my shoes were forced on to my wriggling feet, and then downstairs I went, propelled by a firm hand.

Breakfast was a meal I seldom ate with both parents. My father relished a peaceful breakfast when he was at home – he had told me so. 'Sets me up for the day,' he explained. 'Bad start, bad day. Remember that, Jackie.' He sat with a slice of toast or cup of tea in hand, the morning newspaper obscuring much of his face. Occasionally when a headline caught his attention he commented to my mother who, notepad in front of her, was writing one of her many lists of things to do.

The start of my schooldays marked the end of the calm

time my father had told me he needed. I did try, but my resolve didn't last for long.

My breakfast of a lightly boiled egg and a slice of brown toast was placed in front of me. I pushed it aside. There was something in my throat, something blocking it, and I knew that if I tried to swallow, the food would choke me.

'Jackie, eat your breakfast,' my mother said.

Her face showed no trace of sympathy, only a resigned displeasure at my behaviour. Scared of her disapproval, I forced down some toast, but with the first mouthful I retched. My eyes streamed, I couldn't swallow, and the soggy mess landed back on my plate.

My mother shouted, 'Jackie!'

My father jumped to his feet. 'For God's sake, Dora, do something,' he said tersely. With the paper, he left the room. 'I'll get breakfast on the train,' he called, over his shoulder.

I cringed with embarrassment and fear.

My mother glared at me. 'Well, that's a family breakfast ruined,' she said, and marched me to the downstairs cloakroom. A damp cloth was wiped none too gently across my face, my school dress was inspected for any sign of damage, and all the time her angry voice was buzzing in my ears.

I screamed at her again that I didn't want to leave the house. But I couldn't tell her that my nightmare had stepped out of my sleep and that the fear it brought was sweeping through me. And even if I could have, it would have made no difference. I was going to school and that was that.

I can't remember what happened on the way there or when we arrived. The next thing I do remember was that my mother had gone and I was in a classroom seated at a desk. I sat looking at the door, convinced that somehow I had to reach it and escape.

The teacher turned to write something on the board and I seized my chance. Out of my seat I sprang, and I ran as fast as my feet could take me. Behind me were the images from my nightmare and the echoes of a voice telling me I had to run.

The teacher caught me before I reached the door. She held me against her as I wriggled and cried that I wanted to go home. In the end, unable to pacify me, she picked me up and took me to the headmistress's office. Then there was another voice. It came from the headmistress and eventually calmed me. Gradually my breathing slowed and my fear diminished.

Eventually I was calm enough to be returned to the classroom.

Bottles of milk were passed round, and later we were taken to the school canteen to have our lunch. I was placed next to the teacher and I knew it was because of my behaviour earlier that morning. I didn't mind because she was nice to me and kept trying to include me in conversations. I told her that I liked drawing and she said she would be getting us to do lots of that.

That afternoon we played with sand in the playground before a story was read to us. Just as I was beginning to feel sleepy, a bell rang and my first day at school was over.

After that first day I began to like school – there were days when I raised my hand to answer a question and smiled happily when a word of praise came my way. The teacher tried to encourage me to mingle more with the other children by asking me to pass round books or crayons.

We were each given sheets of paper and told to draw something familiar. 'Why not try and draw the house where you live? Yes, children, let's do that first,' she said, when twenty puzzled little faces looked at her for inspiration.

I drew a large square, then a series of small ones within it to represent windows and the front door.

'Very good, Jackie,' she said. 'Now, who lives in the house?' And again I bent my head to the task. Little stick figures appeared with circles for faces. 'Well done,' she said, to each child in turn, as she walked around the classroom inspecting our work. She stopped at mine. 'Who's that?' she enquired.

'Mummy and Daddy,' I replied.

'No, that one,' she said, pointing to a smaller figure standing apart from the two larger ones.

'That's me,' I answered. She made no comment, but unlike the other children's pictures, which showed groups of figures standing together, I had drawn myself standing alone.

As the days went on I tried to draw animals and flowers as I had seen other children do. Once I drew another house much smaller than the one where I lived. It was in the corner of the page.

'And who lives there, Jackie?' my teacher asked.

'My uncle,' was all I said, and again she made no comment.

I watched as a boy sitting near me drew a big yellow

sun, its rays spreading right across the paper. I reached for the darkest crayon in the box and drew dark clouds followed by dots of rain.

Over the next few weeks our teacher showed us letters of the alphabet, which were placed next to pictures she had pinned up around the room. I tried to stretch my mouth into the required shape and join in with the rest of the class when asked to repeat the sounds she made.

'A is for apple,' we chanted, 'B is for book,' but by the time a picture of a cat was held up, my mind had wandered and the letters were blurred. By the end of the first week of trying to learn the alphabet, I had hardly progressed beyond 'A is for apple'. Simple arithmetic confused me, but when she showed us a large cardboard clock and turned the hands round, I was able to give her the right answers.

We learnt to sing songs and the teacher kept time on a triangle. I tried to remember the words to 'The Wheels On The Bus'. When we heard it start, we all stood up and raised our arms to make circles in the air in imitation of wheels turning. Twenty little bodies swayed to the beat as we sang with more enthusiasm than tunefulness.

But it was drawing I liked best, and gleefully I stuck on the gold stars that showed how well I had done. I was the first child who managed to draw a face with not just a nose and eyes but a bright red mouth full of rather large teeth. For that particular picture I was given more praise. Some of my drawings were pinned to the classroom walls alongside other children's. Others I took home to show my parents. But, unlike my classmates, I knew my pictures would never adorn the fridge or kitchen walls.

At the end of each day, as soon as my coat was on, I would pick up my satchel and go to the gate where my mother was waiting.

'Well, Jackie,' she would say, 'I hope you've been good.' Then, smiling at the other mothers, who were at least a decade younger than her, she would walk slowly away, with me at her side.

'What did you learn today?' was the one question she always asked as soon as my coat was hung up in the hall. I would show her the drawings I had done. 'Very nice, dear,' she would say, before she folded them neatly, then handed them to me to keep in my room.

After the first day I had stopped protesting that I didn't want to go to school. Each morning, after washing and brushing my teeth, I dressed myself in the clean clothes my mother had laid out the night before. I took pride in the fact that, apart from plaiting my hair, I could get myself ready without help. Once breakfast was finished, it was time to leave the house. I would walk beside my mother until we reached the gates, where groups of mothers chatted as they watched their offspring walk into the playground.

But those days, when I knew my mother must have breathed a sigh of relief at my improved behaviour, were not destined to last long.

They dwindled away when my uncle introduced me to his next friend, who, for the first time, came to his house.

8

I never knew the name of my uncle's friend, a chubby little man with twinkling eyes and an easy manner. When I met him, I wasn't scared. Certainly there was nothing about him that would have alerted anyone to what lay behind the pleasant exterior.

'Look, Jackie, I've brought you a present,' he said, as soon as he sat down. His pale, podgy fingers, with a sparkling ring on the smallest one, disappeared inside his jacket pocket and came out holding a small parcel. Inside, there was another soft toy: a pink pig with a key protruding from its side. 'You can add that to your collection,' he said. At the time I didn't question how he knew about the other furry animals my uncle had given me when we played 'the game'.

He showed me how to wind it up and how, once I had placed it on the floor, it ran around in circles. Watching it, I was just a child enjoying a new toy, a child who clapped her hands together with delight. Wanting to share my enjoyment of the pig's antics, I turned to the two adults with a wide smile that lit up my face.

'Pretty little thing, isn't she?' the chubby man said to my uncle, who murmured his agreement. I felt a mixture of shyness and pleasure, as small girls do when they hear a compliment that they know is for them.

I was given some lemonade and, forgetting about the

time when I had been made to drink it, I swallowed it eagerly. Again, it was sweet and syrupy, and just a few sips made me giggle.

The chubby man produced a pack of cards from his pocket. Quickly he shuffled them and then, to my delight, showed me a couple of tricks before laying them down on the table. 'Do you like playing games?' he asked.

Not knowing what was expected of me, I looked at him with growing wariness.

It was then that my uncle mumbled a few words about having forgotten something my aunt had asked him to buy. 'I'd better pop down to the shops quickly, won't be long. You be good, Jackie,' he said. 'Look after my guest.' He left me sitting with a man whose smile never left his face as he explained the game we were about to play.

And as he told me the rules, I clutched Paddington closer to me.

It was called Happy Families but, he explained, he wanted to make it more fun. So when I picked the right card a sweet would come my way. If he picked the right one a kiss would be his reward. But whenever either of us got a wrong card, a piece of clothing was to be removed.

The cards were dealt. Innocuous pictures of bakers, postmen and members of other families smiled up at me. He dealt me another card. It was the right one and, true to his word, he gave me a sweet. But when he dealt the next one to himself, he gave a small triumphant shout. This time he had won. He pulled me towards his seat. 'Kiss,' he said, offering his cheek, and dutifully I did as he asked. I didn't like the feel of his face for he hadn't shaved as closely as my uncle did and the stubble was prickly against my lips.

49

'Now, Jackie, you must take something off.'

I shook my head – and that was when the twinkle left his eyes.

He grabbed me and undid the bow that tied my hair. 'There now – there was no need to make a fuss, was there?'

I wriggled away from him and nervously sipped some more lemonade. The room swam, and I heard him say that I had chosen the wrong card again. It was my shoes that he told me to take off next and my fingers were clumsy as I fumbled with the buckles.

Within the next few minutes, he was down to his vest and underpants.

I stared at my cards to avoid looking at him. I didn't want to see the greying hair that was growing on his chest or the thick blue veins on his white legs – and especially not the outline of something that appeared to be growing in his underpants.

It was when he dealt me another wrong card that he moved. 'Your turn again, Jackie,' he said, and pointed at my dress. 'Put your hands up over your head and I'll help you.'

Reluctantly I did so. It was as though I had no will to protest, no ability to resist. The dress was pulled over my head, leaving me standing in just my white knickers.

They went next, then his underpants – and all I could think of was, Where's my uncle?

He picked me up, cradled me against him, then laid me down on the rug. He rubbed cold ointment of some kind into me before his finger went between my legs and inside my body. I lay there unable to move and it was then that I switched my mind off from my body until I was floating somewhere above it. From there I watched a little girl lying on the floor, her arms held stiffly at her sides and her skinny legs pushed wide apart. I could see her white face, her blue eyes staring blankly at the ceiling as a grey-haired man, with rolls of pale, flabby flesh hanging from his stomach, grunted and groaned with pleasure as he violated her.

It took him no longer to destroy the last shreds of her innocence than it would have done to boil a kettle or toast a slice of bread. To him she was insignificant, merely a vessel for his enjoyment. When he had finished he left her there, a broken doll with her child's white knickers lying where he had thrown them.

The passage of time might have made his features grow faint in my memory, but I can still see his eyes that, once the twinkle had left them, were cold and indifferent, hear his rasping voice – even the smell of him lingers in my memory. I have often thought that if evil has an odour, it was Chubby's. It crawled into my nose, mixed with my tears and left a permanent stain deep within my body's memories. Even now just a tone of voice or a certain laugh brings it back and, once again, my mouth fills with the sour taste of my childhood. Nothing has ever erased it. Chubby is trapped for ever within the labyrinth of my bad memories.

9

That first time when my uncle returned and saw my pale, dry-eyed face – the shock had dried my tears before they had even fallen – he made the chubby man leave.

'You shouldn't have been so rough with her,' I heard him say angrily.

'She'll be all right,' said Chubby, dismissively. 'They always are.'

My uncle picked me up, pushed a small tablet between my lips and held me as I dozed. As I slipped in and out of sleep, his voice kept murmuring how sorry he was. Later he bathed me, then dressed me again. I refused to put on the same clothes that the man had taken off me, so he took my pyjamas out of my overnight bag – the top was patterned with pretty little pink mice – and slipped them on to my torn body.

Why, after what happened that day, did I not talk? I often ask myself that question. But, then, even if I could have formed the words to explain, who would I have said them to? My uncle was the only person who told me he loved me and he already knew about it.

Why did my aunt not question why I was wearing my nightclothes in the late afternoon when she returned from work? And why did she not notice how sleepy I was and how pale? But if she did, she didn't comment and just bustled around as always, making supper and talking about her day at work.

That evening we sat down to chicken and vegetables but the white meat looked dead and the vegetables slimy. I put small morsels into my mouth and forced myself to swallow them slowly, but before I had made any noticeable inroads, I pushed the plate aside. I knew I would vomit if I tried to eat any more.

'What's wrong with you, Jackie? Aren't you hungry?' my aunt asked.

'Oh, leave her alone,' my uncle said quickly, to prevent me replying. 'She'll eat when she's ready.' But I couldn't eat anything else, even when she placed my favourite dessert of apple pie and cream in front of me.

I think we watched television later, because we always did, until it was time for me to go to bed. It was my uncle who tucked me in and placed Paddington in my arms. Clutching my bear, I fell asleep.

It was not long afterwards that my uncle, seeing I had survived the chubby man, told me he would show me what those acts would be like if they were done by someone who cared for me and loved me as much as he did.

Each time my uncle removed my clothes and ran his hands over my body, he whispered endearments before he molested me. I heard his groans of pleasure, followed by his apologies when he knew he had hurt me, and the reassurances that I was loved.

When I was given more of the sweet drinks, I gradually learnt they contained more than lemonade. I saw something from a smaller bottle being added to the fizzy liquid. Whatever was in it made me feel light-headed and woozy, but it took away the pain and the fear.

And every time it happened, the feeling grew that what was taking place was unreal. It took some time but gradually I perfected the process of detaching my mind from my body. Then I, like my uncle, became another observer. That made it seem as though what was happening was happening to someone else.

My nightmares told me otherwise. The disturbing dreams started to visit me more and more often. The images even appeared when I was awake, pictures of writhing adults taking part in grotesque acts, their faces featureless. I would hear a jumble of noises, as though an old cracked recording was playing in my head, issuing instructions. To begin with I couldn't make out what the noises meant, but gradually they turned into voices telling me to run, urging me to escape.

There were times when, as soon as food was placed in front of me, I felt as though something was growing in my throat, restricting it and preventing me from swallowing. No matter how hard I tried, I couldn't dislodge it until I had retched and retched. That was when fear, then anger filled me and threatened to burst through my skin.

In the playground I got into fights with other children. I screamed and punched with little or no provocation. It was only when the teachers came running and pulled me away that I calmed down. At six I was still small enough to control so it was my own safety that concerned them, not their own or even the other children's.

It was when my urge to run became too strong to resist

that they became even more worried. Out of control, my arms swinging and my feet moving as fast as I could make them, I would take off like a sprinter until I reached the school wall, then hurl myself against it with full force. I had realized that physical pain was the only way to stop the inner torment that the nightmares caused. Screaming, I would throw myself against the rough bricks, and the pain of impact would at least stop my thoughts.

Time and again the teachers caught me and I, distraught with tears that streamed down my face, had no memory of who or where I was. As I was held tightly, a high desolate wailing, continuous and piercing, echoed in the school grounds.

10

More little snippets of memory come back to me.

The school strongly recommended, if not insisted, to my parents that I was taken to see a doctor because of my violent outbursts. He would probably refer me to a psychologist, the headmistress explained. There was another serious issue that she wanted to discuss with them: my excessive retching and vomiting. She explained to my mother that, when presented with food or after lunch, I would often be sick. There were no signs that it was self-induced – although I'm sure those adults did wonder. An urgent visit to a doctor was essential, she said. So they arranged to take me first to the local GP, who referred me to a consultant at a hospital in Manchester.

The waiting room was crowded with people – arms in slings, legs in plaster, wheezing and coughing. My mother and I were shown to another room.

'You'll have to get undressed, dear,' the nurse said.

The lights were bright in the small room and I trembled. All I could think of was that somewhere in that room, tucked out of their sight, there was a hidden camera and, behind it, eyes that would watch me.

I shook my head.

She, thinking I was shy, tried to set my mind at rest. 'There's nothing for you to worry about, dear,' she said kindly. 'There,' she said, opening a door, 'is the changing room. I'll be outside with your mummy so no one can see you.' When she noticed that I was still looking at her with distrust, she pointed to something hanging on the inside of the door. 'Look, Jackie, here's a dressing-gown,' she told me – it was a child-sized cotton garment with ties down the back. 'You just slip that on once you're undressed, then knock on the door to tell me you're ready, all right?'

She left me then and, unable to see any sign of camera equipment and reassured that I had something to put on, I hastily undressed and pulled on the dressing-gown.

But I hesitated before I knocked on the door. What were they going to do to me?

Eventually the nurse called me and I walked out. 'That's a good girl,' she said, as she took my hand and led me back to my mother. 'There,' she said brightly, pointing at a chair. 'You sit down and the doctor will see you soon.'

I obeyed, and through the thin fabric of my dressing-gown I could feel the hardness of the plastic chair. I wriggled, trying to get comfortable, and received an irritated look from my mother. 'Keep still, Jackie,' she said curtly, and without replying, I slid down in the chair.

Eyes lowered, I glanced at my mother, wanting her to say something to reassure me that everything was going to be all right. I wanted to hear her say that no one was going to hurt me, but instead she just looked stoically ahead.

The silence seemed to stretch for a long time. I watched the hands on the wall-mounted clock as they moved slowly round and wondered how long we would be kept waiting. At last the nurse came back and said the doctor was ready to see us. We followed her into the room where he was sitting. It was my mother who did all the talking and to her that his questions were directed. There was a brown file in front of him and I saw that my name was written on it.

First he wanted to take my temperature. 'Open wide,' he said. 'I just want to pop this under your tongue.' Instead of complying I pressed my lips tightly together and looked at him fearfully. 'Come on, Jackie,' he said, 'we're only trying to help you!' But still I kept my lips firmly shut. 'Well, Nurse, if she won't let us she won't,' he said, with an exasperated sigh. 'Pop it under her arm, please.' As my pulse was taken and my chest listened to, he and my mother talked over my head. Words like 'hysterical' and 'difficult' were bandied about and the look of sympathy on the doctor's face was directed not at me but at my mother.

'There doesn't seem to be anything physically wrong with her that would cause the vomiting,' he said to my mother, after he had completed the examination. 'I'll write a prescription for something that should calm her.' He took out a pad on which he scribbled something before passing the sheet across the desk to my mother.

Then he looked at both of us and said gravely that he thought he should refer me to someone else. 'Someone who may be able to help her more than I can,' he said, and I heard my mother agree to another appointment being made, this time with a child psychologist.

The next thing I remember is being back in the changing room, getting dressed, and then we were outside, my mother walking briskly and me trotting behind her as I tried to keep up.

I could see her puffs of breath in the cold air as angry words were muttered. 'I just don't know what to do with you, Jackie,' was all she said, once we were in the car.

Being sick, she had decided, was all of my own making, as were the nightmares and my panic attacks.

A week later I was taken to see the psychologist, who composed the first report that is in my file; the one in which it is written that my mother said I had always been a difficult child.

11

I can't remember what the thin man wearing glasses asked me. I only remember that I sat down with a woman he said was his assistant in a room where little plastic shapes were given to me to fit together. After I had done that, I was shown cards with pictures and others with words and asked to put the matching pairs together. Then I had to place bricks with numbers on them in order.

After he had seen what I had done, he left me with his assistant again while he talked to my mother. My reading skills were poor, he wrote, and I was unable to concentrate for more than a few moments. He also wrote that my parents were both concerned and supportive. Between the lines, he summed me up then as a difficult, ungrateful child.

He was the first of the experts I was taken to and he, like those who followed, never looked at the possibility that maybe, just maybe, there was something wrong with my life and not with me. The other doctor had not asked himself why a child should be frightened to open her mouth for a foreign object to be placed in it. Why not? Did many of his other young patients refuse to open their mouths for the thermometer?

Instead they told me how lucky I was, how privileged.

I had everything a little girl could want – toys, pretty clothes, a lovely home and loving parents.

That I do remember because, over the next few years, it was repeated to me time and time again.

12

I have read books about other children, who had been abused by their stepfathers, family members, friends who were in a position of trust, and in some cases even by their own parents. Through their words I learnt how they had coped when a member of their family, whom, until then and often after, they had loved, was their abuser. Often unable to deal with the terrible reality of what was being done to them, these children created two people in their minds: a nice daddy and a nasty one was the most common. The nice one cuddled them and gave presents. The nasty one did unspeakable things.

I did something different: I split the child. Those things were not happening to me, they were happening to her; I only watched and observed. She called to me, that little girl, asked me for help, but I turned away.

It was then that Florence, my imaginary friend, appeared more often. It was she who slid into my bed at night, wrapped her soft arms around me and told me she would stay with me until I went to sleep. In those early years my five-, six- and seven-year-old fantasies did not stop what was happening; they just made it easier to bear.

Through the haze of the world I had retreated into, my mother's voice berated me. She told me she was ashamed of how I behaved: I was an embarrassment to her and my father, and the village was talking about her family. Why was it that I gave my uncle no trouble? Obviously, I could be well behaved when I wanted to be. What had *she* done wrong? What had *she* done to deserve such a difficult child? On and on the list of her grievances went. I shrugged and gave her no answer.

'You've been too busy with your life to see what's wrong with mine,' the voice inside me shouted, but my mother didn't hear it. Instead she sighed with relief when Fridays came, knowing she was free of me until Sunday night.

And I? What did I feel when my abuser took me off in his car and my mother, thinking of the neighbours, dutifully waved us goodbye.

Numb acceptance – for whatever he did, wasn't it him, only him, who also loved and comforted me?

13

As an adult I have asked so often of the child I once was the same question: 'Why did you not talk?' but the child is silent, and I'm left searching for the answers.

When I had read all the books that told me I wasn't alone, that other children had also kept quiet about their abuse, I used the Internet to learn more. I tapped in the words 'abuse' and 'children': page after page came up on my screen.

It was as I read article after article on the subject that I began to understand why children do so little to help themselves. I learnt about how kidnap victims side with the men who have taken them. I read about Stockholm syndrome: it was named after hostages were taken in a bank raid and, after being held at gunpoint for hours, tried to help their captors when they had been freed.

And the more I read, the more I found that when a person guilty of causing pain and distress shows a scrap of kindness, their victim begins to care for and identify with them, that what might have been in the beginning the victim's strategy for survival turns into reality. And when it does, their psyche is warped as they become genuinely sympathetic towards their tormentor.

The most famous of those cases is probably Patty Hearst's. The daughter of a wealthy American family, she was kidnapped by a group of terrorists. She was blindfolded for fifty-seven days, deprived of food and water and sexually assaulted. Yet not only did she try to protect her captors, she later joined them. The pictures of her taking part in a bank raid shocked the world. At her eventual court case her defence was that she had been brainwashed.

As I read those articles, some of my childhood began to make sense: my uncle, over time, had not only created a bond between us but had reinforced it. Although I felt at worst intense hatred and at best a detached indifference towards his friends, he was successful in controlling my feelings towards him. Until I reached my early teens, even though I feared the things he did to me, he could manipulate me into feeling guilty when he pretended I had hurt him.

In my confused mind it was him I needed – for wasn't he the one who comforted me?

After all, I reasoned, as I read the many cases of abuse, if they can control the mind of an adult, what can grown men do to the mind of a child? Certainly after the experience with Chubby, my uncle managed to make a little girl believe that in some way she was to blame, that instead of her being drugged and molested, she was willingly participating in the sexual acts he and his friends were performing on her. But even as I rationalized, I still felt anger towards that little girl, the child who had kept quiet.

For a while after Chubby had raped me, it was just my uncle who molested me and took photo after photo of my naked body. I think he was frightened by the state of shock I had been in after Chubby had left, and that was why he refrained from handing me over to his friends for some time. Instead, he used that time to train me in obedience until he was confident of my silence and compliance. It was then that he constantly reinforced my belief that he was my protector, the one who cared for me most, not my parents.

14

There were two days out of the year that, whether they fell on a weekend or not, I stayed at home. One was my birthday, when I dressed in something new, sat on a chair and waited for my mother's friends to arrive. In a flurry of perfume, air kisses and 'Oh, goodness, how you've grown,' they entered the house bearing brightly wrapped gifts. 'Happy birthday, Jackie,' they said, as they handed over their parcels.

Small sandwiches, their crusts carefully cut off, were passed around, pale sherry was poured into delicate crystal glasses, and orange juice was given to me before I was told to unwrap my presents. Adults, their faces expectant, would watch me carefully. There were books I could not read, dolls I had no interest in, and clothes that were added to my wardrobe. Each item was placed on a tidy pile and the paper they had come in was neatly folded.

'Oh, how lovely,' my mother would exclaim, each time she saw a parcel's contents. 'What do you say, Jackie?' As expected, I would dutifully thank the person who had brought it.

Later the birthday cake was brought in with tiny candles. Not for me something made by my mother with a wobbly 'Happy Birthday' iced on the top, but some magical creation from the speciality cake shop. One year the cake was a blue lake with a small girl skating on it, and another, icing and marzipan were twisted into a bouquet of flowers. I always thought it was a shame when the knife sliced through the cake, scattering crumbs and breaking up the beautiful pictures.

'Blow out the candles, Jackie,' my mother said each year. 'Then you must make a wish.' And I would inhale as deeply as possible, hold it for a second, then blow in one big whoosh. Everyone clapped when the last flame flickered and died, and my reward was being allowed to have the first slice.

Of course, my parents had always given me either the biggest or the most expensive present. I received it as soon as breakfast was finished, and I kept it downstairs to show to the assortment of middle-aged aunties later. The unanimous collective thought always expressed was that indeed I was a very lucky little girl. Before I was ten there was a large wooden doll's house in the corner of my room that I had long ago become bored with; a small gold locket in a drawer of my dressing-table; an eight-track cassette player on a shelf alongside books and videos; a collection of music; more toys than a single child could play with; and an overflowing wardrobe of the latest designs.

The only present that did not have to stay in my room was my bicycle. It was my favourite present, but other than the first day, when it was brand new, it had to be kept in the garage.

The year that there were going to be six candles on the cake, my mother decided I should have a proper party with other children. 'You can invite all your little friends from school,' she said brightly, ignoring the fact that I did

68

not appear to have any and that in the whole year I had been at school I had never been invited to a birthday party.

But my mother was determined that her daughter was going to have a smart party and sent out the invitations. She delivered little printed cards placed in envelopes to the school, for all the children to take home to their parents. She had invited all of my classmates, even the ones I told her I really didn't want.

'Don't be so silly, Jackie,' she said, when I objected. 'Of course we have to include everyone. You can't invite some and not the others.' Even then I knew it was their parents' reactions she was worried about, not the children's.

I don't think it was because they liked me that every child accepted. I think it was more that my mother had put on the invitation that not only were presents unnecessary but that an entertainer had been booked, plus someone to look after the children. All the parents had to do was drop them off and collect them several hours later.

They accepted, as my mother had known they would. After all, what more could a six-year-old's mother wish for than an afternoon to herself, knowing that her child was being well looked after?

The ban on presents was ignored and there were books, for colouring and to read, crayons, and sweets that I was told to share with my 'friends'.

At that first party, while my mother and her close friends were happily sipping sherry and gossiping, we watched a magician do his tricks. Coins appeared from behind small ears, scarves emerged from pockets and, of course, the right card appeared seemingly out of thin air.

The following year, to my mother's delight, invitations appeared for me. At my next birthday party, there was a treasure hunt, and each child found something – but after that one there were no more parties.

By then I was no longer receiving invitations to other children's homes. My increasingly bad behaviour had marked me out not only as a disturbed child but a destructive one as well. Parents warned their children not to play with me, not that they needed warning. By then too many of them had witnessed my bouts of violence and unpredictable behaviour.

'Jackie, I think we should just have a quiet birthday this year,' my mother said firmly. 'Excitement isn't good for you.' So I spent my eighth birthday with her friends. That was the year my aunt and uncle put in an appearance, something they had not done before, preferring to give me their presents when I visited them.

They brought me a huge yellow bear. It was too big to wrap but a large ribbon around its neck made it look like a present.

'Oh, how kind,' my mother said, as usual. 'What do you say, Jackie?'

I looked at the bear, which dwarfed my entire collection, with something approaching repugnance. It was made of nylon and too big, and I didn't think it looked in the least bit friendly. As I gingerly picked it up and heard a growl deep inside it I remembered 'the game' and suddenly felt sick. I swallowed hard in an attempt to hide the fact that bile was rising in my throat. In her own way, my mother had gone to so much trouble that I didn't want to spoil it for her. I knew throwing up on the carpet would certainly do that.

'Thank you,' I said, and pressed my lips to my aunt and uncle's cheeks.

My uncle's presence in my home always made me feel uneasy. I didn't like him being there for, however indifferent my mother appeared to be towards me, it was still the place where I felt safe.

But when my mother invited my aunt and uncle to stay for Christmas, even that little bit of security was taken away from me. 'You can't risk the roadblocks, not if you want to have a few drinks,' she said. On the main roads between the villages there had been a rising number of police enforcing the drink-driving laws. It was expected that, over the festive season, unmarked cars would be parked in the many lay-bys between my uncle's village and ours, ready to pounce on every inebriated reveller. As drinking was something that my parents and their guests enjoyed, alternative arrangements had to be made.

Christmas was the other time I was dressed in my best clothes and told to thank everyone who brought gifts. In the corner of the sitting room there was a huge tree, the green of the branches nearly obscured by the weight of the glittering silver ornaments that my mother brought out each year. Piled high beneath it were the carefully wrapped presents. Some were for the immediate family and other, smaller, ones for friends, who had been invited to my parents' annual drinks and mince-pies party on Boxing Day.

On Christmas Eve I was allowed to stay up later than usual. Just before bedtime my stocking was hung over the stone fireplace, ready to be filled with gifts by Father Christmas.

Family presents were handed out after breakfast; mine were immediately put into my bedroom to join the piles of toys already there.

The year my aunt and uncle came to stay was the one when I received my bicycle. My mother put on Handel's *Messiah*. She played it every year at Christmas. 'It's conducted by Sir George Solti,' she told me, as though the information might persuade me to share her musical taste.

But although I didn't like the music, I liked Kiri Te Kanawa's beautiful voice when it filled our house. But I only remember her because I thought she was pretty, unlike some of the other wobbly lady opera singers I had seen on television.

As soon as breakfast was finished I was told to go and fetch something from the sitting room. It was then I saw it, the dark blue and silver bicycle standing in the corner. Almost breathless with excitement I rushed back into the kitchen.

'You can learn to ride it in here,' my father said – the kitchen was so large that there was plenty of space to manoeuvre a bicycle. I would have liked to throw myself into his arms and tell him I'd wanted one more than anything else, but shyness stopped me and instead I just said, 'Thank you.'

Apart from the bicycle, I can only remember little bits of that day. There were the usual mince pies, dishes of dates, nuts and tangerines, a big tin of Quality Street, and sugared almonds continuously being passed around. It was early afternoon before my aunt and uncle arrived, carrying more presents, bottles of wine and a huge bunch of flowers for my mother.

The usual 'So kind' and 'You shouldn't have' were followed by air-kissing and hugs for me. I can't remember what they brought me or even what other presents I received that year.

I can picture the dining table set for seven people. My parents had invited another couple to join us, a couple around their own age whose grown-up children, like my brother, were spending Christmas with college friends. When they arrived I recognized the long-haired blonde woman. She was the one I had seen in the bedroom with my father that night when they had stayed over. They were introduced to my aunt and uncle, and after drinks we sat down to the meal.

There was a huge turkey with all the trimmings, tiny sausages, mounds of vegetables mixed with chestnuts and piles of roast potatoes. Appreciative remarks from the guests rang out as the bird was brought in for my father to carve. A wing, normally my favourite part, was put on my plate. 'Some breast as well for you, Jackie?' my father said, as he placed a slice of white meat next to it.

It was then that my uncle caught my eye. He smiled the smile that was just for me. I looked hastily down at my plate with its slices of white meat. The pink of the cranberry sauce had started to stain it and suddenly I felt the lump that always stopped me swallowing.

I felt my mother looking at me and put a piece of the meat into my mouth. Please, I said silently to myself, please don't let me be sick. With every scrap of effort I was capable of making, I swallowed it. I drank some juice after each mouthful and somehow managed to get through each course.

My mother scorned paper hats as common, but we pulled the very elaborate gold and red crackers she had ordered from the Harrods Christmas catalogue. The crackers contained only adult gifts – miniature bottles of liqueurs: if you got one you had to drink it, according to my mother. 'I'll have yours, Jackie. I don't think you'll like crème de menthe,' laughed my father, when a bottle of green liquid dropped on to my plate.

'Please can I go to my room?' I asked, once the meal was finished and bottles of port were being opened and poured. I was told I could.

Upstairs I puked up every scrap I had consumed. Despite the warmth from the central heating, I was shivering, covered with gooseflesh. 'Please,' I said to Florence, 'please let him leave me alone.' That night, my Christmas wish was granted: he did.

It was the day after Boxing Day when, tired from two days of eating and drinking, my parents retired early to bed. He came into my room. Even in my sleep, I felt his presence and woke. Without opening my eyes I knew he was standing by my bed. I could hear him breathing, and as I lay completely still, pretending to be asleep, I felt his fingers lightly stroking my face. 'Come on, Jackie, I know you're awake,' he said.

Clutching my duvet, I opened my eyes and looked up at him.

'Miss me?' he asked.

I started to gasp out a warning that someone might hear him, that it wasn't safe, and he, thinking I was trying to protect him, hastened to reassure me. 'Don't worry, Jackie, we're safe. Your parents are exhausted and quite drunk so they'll never wake up. I've told your aunt I was slipping outside for a cigarette – you know what she thinks of me smoking.'

I knew what my mother thought of that as well, but said nothing. I just clutched the covers even tighter around me and wished hopelessly that he would go away.

He flicked off my bedside light but, dim as the room was, I could still see him. 'Have to be quick, though,' he said, and took hold of my head. His fingers buried themselves into my hair as he pulled me forwards while his other hand fumbled with the front of his trousers. The sound of him unzipping them rang in my ears.

He pressed my face against him and, although I tried not to breathe, I still inhaled that sweaty smell and felt hot flesh before he pulled back my bedding and climbed in.

And there in the darkness of my bedroom, where only my teddy bears could see us, he pushed my legs apart and held me tightly until he had finished.

It was after I was sure he had gone, and had heard his soft footsteps retreat as he crept along the corridor to the room he was sharing with my aunt, that I reached up and put my light back on. I avoided looking at my bears – I didn't want to see their eyes, which I knew were watching me.

Instead, I called out to Florence, who crept in beside me, offering words of comfort.

My ghostly pallor the next morning was put down to my having eaten too much rich food over the previous days. 'No more mince pies for you,' someone said.

That Christmas I do remember.

Afterwards the one room that I had thought safe no longer was. The bears now knew my secret and I turned them to face the wall. I didn't want to look into their faces and I no longer wanted to sleep in there. It was Florence, kind, patient Florence, who now comforted me at night. 'Why have you done that with your bears?' she asked, when we were curled up in bed together with her arms around me. And I told her that they had seen what my uncle and I had done.

15

My mother held out a pair of small dark blue knickers and pointed to a mark in the centre of the crotch. I cringed when I saw it, for I knew what it was: a tiny stain that must have escaped my uncle's eagle eyes, for he washed and inspected my underwear whenever I stayed with him.

'Jackie, what's this?' she asked, and behind the question, I heard a note of fear.

'Don't know,' I lied, but my mother and I knew the stain was blood.

'How did it get there?' she asked.

Surely she knew, I thought. There was only one way it could have got there. My mind spun. I knew she was not going to be fobbed off and I searched desperately for something to tell her; something she would believe.

Why did I not tell her the truth? If I'd told her everything, I would have been safe. But that was not something that even entered my head. Just give her something, some half-truth, so she would leave me alone was all I could think of doing.

'I was playing,' I said slowly, trying to find a plausible excuse, 'with one of the boys at school.'

I saw a look of something like relief cross her face but still her mouth was compressed as, grim-faced, she waited for me to continue.

'Go on,' she said, when I made no effort to tell her more.

'You know, games,' I said, into the wall of chilling silence. 'He showed me his willie and I showed him mine.'

'And? Looking doesn't make a stain like this, does it?'

'Well, he . . .' I paused, dreading the consequences of my words '. . . he put his finger inside my pants.'

At those words my mother exploded and her angry words swamped me. I was a dirty little girl, a disgrace to the family; she was ashamed of me. On and on she went, and I stood there shaking. Eventually she told me to go to my room. 'And stay there till I tell you to come out,' she shouted.

I ran up the stairs before she could hurl any more words at me.

'What would she have said if I had told her the truth?' I asked Florence tearfully, but this time she had no answer for me. She just agreed that if I had, my uncle was right, we would be in very bad trouble.

That was the start of a new period of my life. In my parents' eyes my behaviour significantly worsened. Now I no longer wanted to be in my room and tantrums occurred each time I was told to get ready for bed.

I fought off sleep, with its associated nightmares, for as long as possible.

And when eventually, unable to battle against my eyes closing, I entered the room where the little girl was, her fear became mine. My eyes would fly open and I would find that the air in my room was threatening to suffocate me.

That was when I started pulling my bedclothes off and,

half asleep, I would take them on to the landing. There, I would curl into a tight ball and fall back to sleep.

It was my father who found me the first time. 'Jackie, what are you doing?' he asked, as he picked me up and carried me back to bed.

The first time he was not angry but when I was found there time and time again, both parents were. Was I sleep-walking, they asked, as they looked in despair at the child who was showing even more signs of disturbance.

It was not much longer before they found me hunched in a corner of my bedroom, thumb in mouth, eyes tightly shut, rocking back and forth.

They called to me, but I didn't hear them. They touched me and my eyes flew open as I cringed away from them. But, locked in another world, I stared blankly into space.

At school things were no better. The headmistress contacted my mother to tell her that again I had run out of the classroom, screaming with rage, and thrown myself against the outside wall. When, fearing I would hurt myself, the teachers had tried to restrain me, I had hit out furiously at them until my panic was spent.

When I was picked up and carried to the headmistress's office, I started to cry, that long, high-pitched, desolate wailing, continuous and piercing. And even when I had calmed down there was, my parents were told, a detachment about me, as though I did not recognize either my surroundings or who was with me. There was talk then that maybe another school, one that catered for problem children in a residential environment, might be better for me. But my mother, unable to accept the stigma of an unstable daughter, had persuaded the school that I should stay at home.

Another visit to the psychologist followed, but again no conclusions were reached as to *why* my behaviour had deteriorated to such an extent. 'Regression,' they said, but they were wrong: it was not as simple as that, for I had no memory of those brief times when I became my toddler self. I read about it much later when the psychiatrists helped me understand my condition and what had happened. I had not just regressed: I was conjuring up the toddler I had been before everything that happened, happened. And once I had done that, I felt safe and could slip back into being her.

It must have been around then that my mother started to question if I was ever going to get better. I sensed fear in her – fear of my actions and fear of the disgrace that a mentally ill child might bring to her family and her own standing in the community.

But even she could not visualize exactly what the following years would make me capable of.

My mother, I knew, looked forward to the weekends when the house no longer rang with my tantrums and despair. Uncle was so kind, so good and so helpful, she told me. And every Friday she and I waited for the person who still said he loved me to come and take me away.

It was then, faced with my mother's despair, the school's opinions and the inability of the psychologists to diagnose me, that my father decided they should take me away. Then perhaps something might change.

16

'We're going to northern Spain for our summer holiday,' he announced, a few days before school was due to break up. He had bought a cottage there after falling in love with the area on one of his many business trips.

Not for him an apartment near the popular beach areas, which were only just beginning to be fashionable, but a large old stone *finca* where lemons and avocados grew in the garden.

'The real Spain,' he said.

I had already gleaned from conversations I had over-heard that my mother was disappointed at not being near the beach.

'Oh, Dora, you wouldn't like it there. Where there are decent beaches there are tourists all summer long. Cheap package tours from Ireland and Manchester,' he added, for greater emphasis, to my class-conscious mother. 'Factory workers all booking into self-catering accommodation and bringing hordes of noisy children with them.' My mother capitulated. 'No, we're going to stay in the real Spain,' he said.

'When are we going?' she asked, with a smile that excluded me. 'We have to make arrangements for Jackie.'

'That's the whole point, Dora. Jackie's coming with us. This holiday is for her.'

I guessed that arrangement had not pleased my mother.

From other conversations I surmised that my father thought taking me to a completely different environment for the whole of the summer might help me. That was the reason he had taken more than two months off work. Being away from home so often might be a factor in my bad behaviour and he wanted to try to help. 'I know everything has been your responsibility, so I thought it was time for me to see what I could do for her, Dora,' I heard my father say.

Peeping round the door, I heard my mother, with a glass of wine in her hand, say she didn't know what she would do if this didn't work out.

'It's all right for you,' she said. 'You're away so much, but I'm here with her all the time. The other parents pity me. Me! There's never been anything like this in our family.'

I heard the glug of more liquid being tipped into a glass as another drink was poured. Then her voice started to rise: 'I just don't know what's wrong with her. And, what's more, I don't think those damn psychologists that the school keeps telling me to take her to do either. She just sits there and looks blank when they ask her questions and I can't read her mind.'

My father made some sounds that were meant to comfort her but my mother had burst into floods of tears. 'I just don't know what to do any longer,' she said.

'She's too young to diagnose, Dora,' my father said quietly. 'They've told us that. We can't just give up on her.'

I knew from his tone that whatever was wrong with me was making him sad, and that worried me. I had heard the mutters at school and seen children raise a finger to the side of their heads – I knew they meant I was crazy. At six I had just known that school scared me, but as I became a little older the fear that there was something wrong in my head began to torment me.

I heard my mother protesting. That was not what she'd meant, she said, but she was at the end of her tether – more wine sloshed out of the bottle. Wine, I had learnt, was something to be drunk when an adult was at the end of her tether, or after a bad day at his office. But then again it seemed to be equally popular on evenings when everyone had a good time. It was a discrepancy that puzzled me.

'Come on, let's try this, Dora. Maybe if we're all together away from here, it might help.'

'You're right, of course you are. I just thought a holiday without her would give me a rest.'

So she doesn't want me to go, I thought angrily and, fearful of being caught listening, I tiptoed away.

My father waited until the next morning to tell me his news. We had finished breakfast and the plates had been cleared away. He leant forward and said, 'Jackie, your mother and I have got something exciting to tell you.' Pretending I knew nothing about it, I looked enquiringly at him.

'We're going to Spain,' he said. 'For the whole of your summer holidays.'

Spain was a word. That was all it meant to me at that age. But it did not take my father long to paint a picture of what it was like, and he told me how much I was going to enjoy myself.

He told me about the village where we were going – it had not changed for a hundred years – and how friendly the people who lived there were. He described the old cottage he had bought and how, from the windows, we could see the lemon groves. He talked about the mountains and the sparkling streams that ran down them and the rivers that flowed to the sea. 'There's even a stream running right through the land our cottage is built on and just a short distance away there's a forest full of pine trees. The air is perfumed with their scent. We can smell it from the bedroom windows.' He told me enthusiastically about how we were going to go on the ferry, then drive through France into Spain as soon as school broke up for the summer holidays. I could feel him trying to get a spark of interest out of me as I sat expressionless at the table.

'We're not going in a plane, then?' I finally asked, because I knew some of the other children in my class had travelled to other countries in one. That was something I did think might be exciting.

He laughed. 'No, Jackie, we're going to drive. You'll see a lot more that way. You only get to see clouds when you fly and a tarmac strip when you land. Remember, I do it all the time on business and it isn't very exciting at all. Anyhow, we couldn't take your bike on a plane, could we? And I thought you and I could do some exploring.'

'But you haven't got a bike,' I said, with a child's logic.

'Well, Jackie, I'll get one.'

I knew by my mother's silence that exploring was not something she was going to join in with but, hearing my father's words, I felt something like a warm glow. The holiday plans had captured my mother's and my imagination and from then on my father was bombarded with questions.

'But do they speak any English where we're going?' my mother asked, and was told he didn't know because he had only spoken to them in Spanish.

My father was fluent in French and Spanish. He did business in South America, and had learnt the language from a box of self-study cassettes.

'It's not difficult to learn, Dora – I still have the tapes,' he tentatively told her. Curtly she replied that she had no intention of going back to studying at her age, so she would just have to rely on him; that idea seemed to please him.

For once I looked forward to school breaking up, and the day after term ended, our large family car was loaded with cases and we were ready to set off. Shorts, sandals and cotton T-shirts, plus a couple of warm jumpers, were all we would need, my father said. But this was something that my mother appeared to have forgotten when she put her things ready to go into the car. I saw a large suitcase, a makeup bag almost as big as the case she had packed for me and a box of glossy magazines and books.

I was allowed to bring Paddington. I had been given some swimming trunks for him one birthday, and with a pair of children's sunglasses, he was ready for a summer holiday too. I also packed his little flowered pyjamas – a duffel coat and wellington boots would be too warm in that climate.

'Bring some books as well,' my father had said. I brought colouring ones only – I still found reading difficult.

I have only a fuzzy image of that long drive and finally

entering the village. We had stayed overnight in France, but by the time we reached the end of our journey I had fallen asleep on the back seat, surrounded by luggage.

I drowsily opened my eyes to see dark shadows move across the sky as the clouds shifted through the silvery light of the moon. It splashed on to the long, single-storey building that was going to be our home for the next few weeks. It was very silent and still. I could smell the sharp perfume of the lemon trees and the pines, as my father had promised.

He carried me inside. 'Let's put her straight to bed,' he said. I heard him say softly to my mother that I'd looked so peaceful when I was asleep that he hadn't wanted to wake me, and for once I smiled up at him and allowed myself to be carried into a bedroom.

My mother helped me pull on my nightclothes, covered me with a blanket and left me.

I woke the following morning to piercing sunlight shining through the windows and a feeling almost of well-being. Impatient to see what was outside, I leant out of the window to inspect my new surroundings.

During the night a light wind had chased away any lingering clouds, leaving a vast expanse of clear blue sky. The brightness of the morning lured me into wanting to leave the house.

I could see small trees with their bright yellow fruit, and in the distance, there were fields of lush green grass. Scattered with the red and yellow of wild flowers, they covered the ground all the way to the lower slopes of the green and grey backdrop of the mountain range.

The morning warmth and the view from my window

began to uncoil the knots of fear that constantly tightened in my stomach. The remnants of the nightmares disappeared as I pushed the window wider and breathed in the smells of jasmine, pine and fresh air. Suddenly the sunlit morning whispered to me of being a free child again – of playing in those fields and of not being afraid.

My father came into my room, smiling to see me enjoying the view. He told me to get dressed, and that as soon as I had had breakfast, he was taking me to buy groceries while my mother had a lie-in.

We walked down a path that took us through the orchard of lemon trees to the village, which was just a few cobbled streets lined with whitewashed houses. It was so different from our village, with its stone houses where net curtains hid the interiors from view. Here, window-boxes, blazing with bright pink and red geraniums, adorned every freshly painted sill. The combined scent of garlic, herbs, freshly baked bread and coffee floated out of every kitchen.

All around us I could hear speech I couldn't understand. Round-hipped matrons chatted in the streets as their children played with homemade toys. Old women sat in open doorways, their legs hidden by long black skirts, knitting needles clicking as busy fingers turned balls of soft wool into garments. Their faces broke into smiles as they saw us. '*Hola*,' they said, and my father smiled back as he greeted them in the same language.

We stopped at the bakery and bought rolls, then walked on to another shop where my father piled his basket high with spicy chorizo sausage, thick slices of ham and a dozen freshly laid eggs. Then he took me to a small café.

'We can have our morning coffee together, Jackie,' he said, and I rewarded him with a sudden smile.

'*Dos café con leche, por favor*,' he said to the man who came out to greet us.

'What's that mean?' I asked.

'Oh, nothing complicated,' he said. 'I just ordered two white coffees. I think you're old enough to try coffee, don't you?' And sitting outside at the small pavement café, with the already hot sun high overhead, my father beside me in an open-neck shirt and denim jeans, I drank my first ever cup of the strong milky brew. With each sip, I thought I had never tasted anything so delicious.

It was later that day that I met some of the village children. Maybe it was because I did not speak their language or they mine that it was easy to play with them. I saw nothing but friendly interest on their faces as, using sign language, they showed me their games. Throwing and catching a ball, tossing stones in the air and seeing how many we could catch on the back of our hands, and flicking dried peach stones into small holes were the most popular.

These village children had no need of expensive toys, I learnt. The only thing they envied was my bicycle – they all wanted one. When I left the house friendly children's voices called out to me, '*Hola*, Jackie!' and by the end of the first week I was yelling, '*Hola*,' back to Pedro, Maria or Antonio.

It was during those first few days that, true to his word, my father took me exploring in the forest. To get there we walked through the village and crossed the bridge, which I leant over to see the plump, silvery, speckled brown fish that swam in the clear water. When we entered the forest I saw squirrels hiding behind trees and found myself laughing as they played hide and seek.

Above our heads thick green foliage nearly obliterated the rays of the sun. My father led the way to a glade where the stream flowed and the trees grew more thinly. Dancing spangles of light shone through the leaves and the only sounds that disturbed the peace were the buzzing of a cloud of midges and the burping of frogs. My father had brought sandwiches and, sitting by the stream where pale green fronds of thickly growing ferns trailed in the water, we ate them contentedly, washing them down with cool drinks.

It was in the glade that I saw the golden eagle.

It was my father who spotted the huge bird and he gently touched my shoulder. 'Jackie, just look at him,' he said, pointing towards the sky. Following the direction of his finger, I watched the majestic bird, its wing span appearing longer than our arms, soaring high, a freshly caught small rodent hanging from its talons. With our heads tilted back we followed its flight until, entering a crevice in the mountain, it was lost from view.

That for me was the highlight of the day and it is a memory I carry with me. That bird had the freedom to fly above the world. How many times would I try to do that too, to escape my demons?

There were days when I rode my bicycle but I never got very far as the olive faces of the children smiled at me. They ran after my bike, their hands took mine, and they brought me to a halt and into their play. We went to the outskirts of the village where we would climb over gates. Feet sank into the droppings of cows and sheep, wild roses' thorns tore clothes and scratched arms and legs as we ran across the fields into the dense woods. Exhilarated by the thought of the adventures that lay ahead, we ignored what would later get us into trouble with our mothers. The sun tanned my face and whitened my hair, while the wind put a rosy glow in my cheeks. We swam in the streams, climbed trees, daring each other to go higher, and with our legs dangling from a protruding branch, we sat watching for wood pigeons and buzzards. But I never saw the eagle again.

Our *finca* was a four-bedroomed cottage where the kitchen, with its low wooden beams and huge black wood-fired stove, took up nearly all of the downstairs. It was where we gathered to eat, read and talk, and it was there that my mother, glass of red wine in hand, would cook our evening meals.

Even she seemed more relaxed, and at night we sat in the large room or in the shady garden simply watching a sunset before I would crawl into my bedroom to sleep. Exhausted by the outdoor life and by being able to behave like a normal child, my sleep was dreamless and undisturbed.

When my mother protested that she was tired of cooking, my father drove us to an old restaurant where we were served small dishes of *tapas* – olives, little squares of cheese, fish that was brought in daily from the coast less than thirty miles away, and a thick omelette made with potatoes and vegetables. On Sundays we liked going there and watching the noisy groups of large extended Spanish families consume vast dishes of paella.

It was on one of those days that we were invited to what the Spanish called a *fiesta*.

'You have to see it,' my father told us, despite my mother's reticence. We watched women and girls dressed in long skirts and tight-fitting blouses, with silver hoops shining in their ears, walk beside men wearing stone-coloured trousers and waistcoats. Dark blue berets were perched jauntily on the men's and boys' heads while white scarves covered the long hair of the women. Small children, pushing and jostling, ran beside them and, feeling the atmosphere, we followed them to the grounds outside the restaurant where the festivities were taking place. Not only was everyone from the village attending but all the outlying areas seemed to be represented too.

Bright rugs had been thrown on to the grass, turning the area into a tapestry of colour. Baskets of food were unpacked, wine opened and the afternoon's fun began.

Ignoring the fact that I had just eaten a large plate of rice and seafood, I took the proffered fresh crusty bread and a slice of the dark red spicy chorizo. I munched on it contentedly, as everyone else did, and waited for the music to begin.

That Sunday afternoon when the sun beat down from a cloudless sky, the young couples and the youth of that mountain area drank wine and ate dishes of cheese and meat. They smiled, laughed and flirted as they chatted, while wiry old couples, their skins burnished to mahogany from their years of toil in the fields, sat on thick cushions, their backs propped against tree-trunks. Blue-veined hands lay loosely on bony knees as they drowsily watched the festivities through half-closed eyes.

One by one the musicians picked up their instruments. The first placed the *txistu*, a small black flute, to his lips, which sent a delicate pure sound floating into the air. Then the fingers of two of the men with him strummed against the taut skin of the tambourines. Batons were beaten against drums before the accordion added its rousing sound. A girl, no more than eighteen, joined them. Her fingers clicked, her body moved and then she started to sing. Hers was a high, sweet voice that at first sent just a few notes shimmering across the field. The tempo increased, until the full sound of the *jota* rang out bringing the audience to their feet. Almost as one, men and boys held out their hands to their partners.

The long skirts of the girls, some of whom had barely become women, swished as hips swayed to the music's hypnotic pulse.

Their mothers, waistlines thickened by middle age, moved their bodies in time to the beat. Hands clapped to the rhythm, backs became erect, heads straightened, fingers clicked, and the eyes of the girls they had once been shone out of creased faces as their feet involuntarily took up the familiar dance steps. Dressed in miniature Basque costumes, children who had only just learnt to walk swung non-existent hips and stamped tiny feet in imitation of their elders.

My new friend Maria's older sister, with strands of her black curly hair escaping from her white headscarf, entered the dance. Her full skirt swirled showing flashes of white stocking-clad legs. Her feet flew in their soft slippers and she was spinning in time to the music. With her arms raised and her fingers snapping, she performed the jumps and kicks of the dance with one of her many young admirers.

'Come on, Jackie, you can do it,' she called, in heavily

accented English when she saw me standing on the sidelines. Needing no more encouragement, I joined in.

I saw my mother as I had never seen her before, her head thrown back looking up at my father, her smile bunching up her face and her eyes shining. He pulled her to her feet, placed his arms around her waist and spun her in time to the music but, try as he might to copy the graceful steps of the Spanish men, he looked exactly what he was: a tall, lanky English visitor, with little sense of rhythm but intent on enjoying himself. The Spanish clapped and applauded them, and with one more wild spin, my parents collapsed on the ground, laughing. Seeing them like that, I felt a wave of love and trust. If only we could stay in Spain, I thought, everything would be fine – but of course we couldn't. And it wouldn't.

Later my father played *pelota*, with a long wicker racquet, in a makeshift court with all of us children. Near the end of the day I watched as the cone-shaped brightly coloured papier-mâché *piñatas* were filled with sweets before being strung up on wires suspended from posts. We younger ones were each given a long stick.

'You have to try and hit them, Jackie,' my father explained. 'When it breaks the sweets will fall out and you get to keep the ones you manage to pick up. Come on.' He took my hand and led me nearer to the target.

Other fathers were placing blindfolds over their children's eyes but my father saw panic on my face when he tried to do the same. 'It's all right, Jackie,' he said soothingly. 'As you're a visitor you don't have to wear one.' He led me into the midst of the activities.

We squealed with excitement when a stick connected

with its target. With loud cracks, the papier-mâché broke and a shower of brightly wrapped sweets fell to the ground. Shouting with delight, we gathered as many as we could find and crammed them into mouths and pockets before joining our families to show them our spoils.

Once the sky became streaked with the orange and red of sunset, we knew it was time to go home; rugs were gathered up, baskets packed, children marshalled and reluctant teenagers urged to say their goodbyes.

That was near the end of our holiday and the final days sped by until it was time to leave. I said goodbye to all my new friends in the village and said I would be back next year. I promised to try and learn more Spanish by then. I did not know as we packed up the car that none of that would ever materialize.

17

We arrived back from Spain a week before school was due to start. My uncle remained curiously silent and I was not sent to stay with him.

Each day I took out my bicycle and rode it off the estate till I reached the country lanes. Pedalling along them, I could feel the wind on my face, and smell the scent of freshly cut fields and grass. But I missed Spain, the friendliness of the people, the children I had played with and, most of all, I missed how we had at last seemed like a family and how my parents had treated me while we were there.

I consoled myself with the thought that I was going back again next year. And in the meantime I had so many stories to tell the other children at school. My father had taken photographs and he gave me an extra set of my own. There were some of our cottage that showed the lemon trees, part of the village and the surrounding countryside. But mainly they were photos of me. There I was, happy and tanned in a group of laughing children, dancing at the *fiesta*. Another showed me riding my bike, a smile lighting my face as my father called to me to look up at him, and others where I was simply enjoying playing with my friends. Those pictures were already in my satchel ready to show to everyone once the new term started, and the stories that accompanied them were locked in my memory.

If I had those photographs now they would show how my holiday had distanced me from those images of my uncle and what he made me do. They would demonstrate that, without his presence in my life, I could have been a normal child.

That realization came to me when I was a teenager and looked at them again. It was why, in a blind rage at the unfairness of the world I lived in, I tore them into little pieces. But that came later, and with it, the second part of my story.

For six lovely weeks there had been no teachers shouting at me, no doctors appraising me sternly from across their desks. My mother had ceased to give me those cold glances, tempered with worry and dislike; instead, there had been moments when she had shown me genuine warmth.

And my father had told me that he just wanted me to be well. His face had lost the concerned expression it so often wore when he looked at me.

Last, there had been no uncle with his camera.

18

It was my bicycle, gleaming with polish, that found me a new friend. Concentrating on rubbing the chrome trim, I didn't see the girl until she spoke.

'Hey, cool bike!' said a voice, and looking round, I saw a girl leaning over our wall.

We eyed each other for a few moments, she with a friendly expression, and me with a puzzled one because I had never seen her before.

'Hang on,' she said. 'I'll come round.' Cloth in hand, I waited for her to appear, which, wheeling her bike, she did a few minutes later. 'I'm Kat,' she said. 'We moved in while you were away.' That explained why I hadn't recognized her. She was a couple of years older than me, tall for her age, and like me, she was dressed in shorts and a T-shirt. Her dark hair was tied into a high ponytail, her eyes were brown and her face was lightly freckled by the sun.

'I've seen you around,' she said offhandedly. 'If you're going for a ride, do you mind if I tag along?'

'Suppose,' I answered, hiding my pleasure at being singled out.

Being older, she rode in front. Her slim tanned legs pumped furiously, and her ponytail swung, as she half stood on her pedals to gain extra momentum. Occasionally, just to check I wasn't too far behind, her head would swivel round and she would grin at me. 'Can't keep up, then?'

At the challenge, my head went down and, like her, I stood on my pedals and urged the wheels to turn faster.

She showed me how, when we were at the top of the hill, to kick my legs off the pedals and freewheel down. When there was a bump in the road we both crouched over our handlebars so that the wheels almost left the ground.

When we stopped to rest, I learnt that her parents were divorced and that her mother had recently remarried. 'Dad's got a new girlfriend too. But she takes me shopping and lets me choose what I want – all goes on Dad's credit card, of course,' she said, with a laugh.

She didn't like her mother's new husband. 'Oh, he's nice enough to me, but I know he wishes I'd go and live with my father. I heard him talking about sending me to boarding school the other day. And he always calls me Kathleen not Kat. My real dad calls me Kitty. Stupid, eh?' I sensed that, underneath, she liked it.

Nonchalantly she pulled a packet of cigarettes out of her shorts pocket. 'Pinched them,' she said airily. 'They never notice,' she added, as she lit one and inhaled. A plume of smoke drifted above her head and my eyes opened wide. Smoking was banned in our house – 'A filthy, dirty habit,' my mother said repeatedly. Friends and my uncle were sent to the garden to indulge in what she called 'their addiction'.

Not wanting Kat to think I was a baby, I stretched my hand out for one.

'You've not smoked before, have you?' she teased.

'Have so,' I answered defiantly as I took one. I put it into my mouth, took the box of matches, struck one and, as I had seen her do, sucked in the smoke. As it went down my throat, I coughed and spluttered. Tears ran down my cheeks as I tried to draw breath and I could hear Kat's laughter.

I don't know what grown-ups see in this, I thought, as a wave of nausea rose from my stomach.

'Cool,' was what I said, as soon as I could get the word out, and by the end of the afternoon, although careful not to inhale again, I was puffing away like an expert.

That was the beginning of our friendship, in which she would introduce me to her taste in music and later tell me the facts of life – or, rather, her version of them. Little did I know that both would get me into trouble with my mother.

My mother, pleased that I had made a friend, even if she was a little bit older, was friendlier to me for the first few weeks after we arrived back from Spain.

'Can I stay at home this weekend?' I had asked, the first time my uncle invited me to visit. And on that occasion they told me of course I could: not only had I found a friend but I also had things to get ready for my new term at school.

Loitering near an open door, I heard my parents talking about me. 'Maybe she's going to be all right now,' I heard my father say, as though what had been wrong with me was no more serious than a cold that a few weeks in the sun had cured.

My mother, I could tell by her reply, was not as optimistic: 'We'll have to see, Stewart. Let's just hope so.'

A week after school had started, my mother announced that my uncle was picking me up and that I would be spending the weekend with him and my aunt as usual. 'He said it's so long since he's seen you and he's really looking forward to it, Jackie,' she said, when she saw my face fall.

I had wanted to take my bike out again and ride in the countryside with Kat. I dreaded seeing him but knew that arguing would get me nowhere. I had seen the fridge full of groceries, heard telephone calls: my parents were planning one of their dinner parties. I also remembered what I had seen before and knew from the odd snippet of conversation that that was why they wanted me out of the way. Although I still did not understand exactly what wife-swapping meant, I had some idea of what happened on those evenings.

Once when I had returned from my uncle's house I found a used condom under my bed. I might not have known what it was but I recognized the smell when I threw it away. My mother had changed the bedding but must have forgotten to check under the bed. I wondered which of her friends had been in it.

The realization of why I was being sent away enraged me. If the holiday had helped me, it had not changed anything, or how my mother really felt about me. I was, I began to understand, an inconvenience to her and her way of life, something that could be farmed out to relatives when it suited her.

19

When the bell announcing that school had finished for the day rang on Friday, the sounds were always different from other days. There was the excited chatter of children who had the weekend free. As they scampered to the gates, they shouted plans of what they were going to do and made arrangements to meet up with best friends. I walked slowly across the playground. I was in no hurry to go home and hear my mother greet my uncle before turning to me with one of her bright smiles as she said goodbye.

He was waiting for me as I walked through the school gates. 'I couldn't wait to see you, Jackie,' he said, as he leant over and opened the car door.

He offered his cheek and I gave it a peck. A chaste kiss between uncle and niece in a public place that could not have offended even the most prudish observer. 'How well you're looking,' he exclaimed, and gradually, as it always did, his charm began to cast a spell over me. It was not the spell of love or even admiration, but the spell of need. My need to have someone in my life who said I was the most important person in theirs.

We went back to my house where I picked up my already packed case and listened to my mother telling me to be good. Every time the car slowed, my body clenched – I was frightened that he would turn off towards one of his friends' houses. But to my overwhelming relief we just went straight back to his.

That weekend he played the part of caring uncle and took me out for the day to the closest northern city, with its large shops and restaurants. 'Is there anything you would like?' he asked, when we went round one of the department stores.

Unable to think of anything I needed, I shrugged. Undeterred by my seeming indifference, he chose something I really did want: a Walkman. I had seen the portable cassette player complete with earphones advertised in the paper and in magazines, sported by attractive young adults and teenagers. The thought of owning one was exciting but still I maintained the 'cool' demeanour I had learnt from Kat.

'You can take it out with you when you go cycling,' he told me. 'Just don't wear it when you're on the road. You won't be able to hear the traffic if it's loud.' Promising him I wouldn't, I took hold of my latest present.

Our next stop was a music shop where he allowed me to wander around the aisles and choose whatever I wanted. He said there was no point in having a player without the cassettes. Kat had mentioned a couple of singers she liked so, not knowing much about pop, I chose cassettes by them. Finally, we ended up at one of the new hamburger bars – McDonald's – where, perched on a red plastic stool, I happily consumed a large hamburger with chips and a creamy strawberry milk shake. Then we went back to his house to spend an evening in front of the television with my aunt.

For the rest of that weekend he never referred to his

previous actions and just talked about Spain, what I had seen and done there.

It was on the drive home on the Sunday evening that he told me he and my aunt were taking a two-week holiday. 'We have ours at the end of the summer, once the schools have gone back. It's quieter then,' he said.

Somehow, although he hadn't touched me and had said nothing about what had taken place before, I was not lulled into feeling safe. Instead, over the time he was away, I felt apprehensive. Even then, I instinctively knew that he had no intention of stopping. I wondered what he had in store for me.

But however suspicious I was at nearly nine, I was not mature enough to fathom why he had given no hint of his feelings for me, or why he had just acted as a middle-aged man should towards his niece. He had not changed: he was simply biding his time. My uncle had other plans for me, and he wanted to make sure that, after being away from him for two months, I was still going to comply with them. He could not have found that out in one day.

20

Three weeks later my suspicions were confirmed. I was sent by my parents to stay at my uncle's house again. There, on his home territory, he used reminders of past deeds, warnings of what would happen should anyone find out, and reassurances that he would always look after and protect me to keep me ensnared in the web he had woven.

It only took him a couple of weekends to have me where he wanted me.

Once he was sure that I was once again in his power, Chubby returned. It must have been some time in October because I remember my mother referring to the warm days we were having as an 'Indian summer'. It was late morning and my uncle and I had taken chairs outside into the garden and were sitting companionably near each other in the sunshine. I had my headphones on, listening to music, and was sipping from a glass of Coke he had poured for me.

I was daydreaming about Spain while he was reading his newspaper.

There was nothing in his demeanour that morning to warn me of what he had planned, so when the doorbell rang I wasn't alarmed.

My uncle went to answer it, then called out to me: 'Come into my office, Jackie. We have a visitor.'

At those words the old dread returned. I walked in to

find the man whose face I had tried unsuccessfully to block from my mind.

'Hallo, Jackie,' he said, as he sat down near to where I was standing. I felt my legs turn to jelly. 'Remember me?' From the look of fear on my face he knew that, of course, I did.

This time there were no presents, no card tricks to entertain me and no twinkling eyes. Just a short fat man, who sat with his ample legs splayed and pulled me towards him while, in a flat, expressionless voice, he told me what he wanted to do to me.

He was so close to my face that he breathed his sour breath into my mouth with every word he spoke. 'Now, then,' he said, 'this time you're going to show me your bedroom.'

I looked at my uncle for help but he turned away and I knew that Chubby's arrival had been planned and that no assistance would come from him.

Fat fingers prodded me in the direction of the door leading into the main house. As I stumbled through it, and up the stairs to the bedroom that was mine when I stayed, I could hear him wheezing behind me. But not a word was spoken.

As we entered the room he closed the curtains, cutting out the bright sunlight and the likelihood of being observed by prying neighbours.

He then turned his attention to me and removed my clothes. My dress was yanked over my head; my knickers were pulled down until I was wearing only my sandals. 'Take them off,' he said.

Bending down, I undid the straps and slowly set them aside, feeling giddy as I raised my head.

Chubby, I came to realise, knew the weakness of little girls who had reached the age of being shy about anyone seeing their naked bodies. He knew that the humiliation he could inflict on me would have an even greater effect than the pain of the act. It was the humiliation, as well as the thinly disguised threats – oft-repeated ones that the child would be blamed should they ever be discovered – that ensured silence. Also, to speak out would mean having to relive those moments of degradation.

I was like a rabbit caught in the headlights of a car. It must know when it sees the huge metal machine hurtling towards it that if it doesn't move it will be crushed. But, transfixed by the lights, the rabbit waits for its inevitable fate. I, too, did not have either the will or the strength to refuse to do what was expected of me. I knew by the expression on his face that, should I try, his delight in making me would give him even more pleasure.

So I did everything he told me to.

'Stand there,' he said, moving the pillows and lifting me on to the bed, pushing my back against the brass rail. 'Now spread your legs wide.'

My uncle came in with the camera equipment and I shivered as he set up the tripod. A light shone on my face as Chubby instructed me to touch myself. Then, leaving his shirt on, he pulled off his trousers, climbed on to the bed and made me sit on him. Underneath my small frame with his hands holding me firmly in place he jerked and grunted. 'Uh, uh,' he groaned. The sounds gradually became higher-pitched and louder as they climbed the scales of his ecstasy, and his fat body shook with shudders. He tossed me off him then and I lay dry-eyed in a small, crumpled heap.

It was when he had finished that, for the first time, I was slapped. I bit my lip to stop myself crying out as his large ring-covered hand slammed against my bottom. He laughed when he saw me wince. 'You'll learn to like that soon,' he said. 'Pain can become pleasure.' With those words, which I was to hear more times than I want to remember over the next five years, he stood up and got dressed.

'Now it's your turn,' he said to my uncle, and then it was Chubby who took over directing the camera.

After the fat man had gone, he couldn't resume the charade that he was the loving uncle and I the child who was dependent on him. I went silently back outside to the garden. He did not try to cajole me. He was not worried that his power over me was diminishing. He knew as well as Chubby did that any chance of my talking was now past: I was far too ashamed to confide in anyone. I could never choke out the words to describe my pain or the nightmare I was living in once again.

I sat on the grass, my arms hugging my knees. The place between my legs throbbed with pain and my mind replayed the images of what they had done to me.

When I had gone into the house earlier, I had left my half-drunk glass of Coke outside. Several wasps had crawled into it. Some were already dead, but others were struggling to climb out up the slippery surface of the glass. But their bedraggled wings only pulled them round in circles so I picked up the glass and turned it upside-down.

Then I took the newspaper that my uncle had left open on the chair and held it out for them. One by one they crawled on to it and the paper started to absorb the liquid that held them down. As they dried and recovered they slowly worked their wings, before flying up towards the warmth of the sun and freedom.

That day, my time in Spain became only a distant memory. It was the end of the chance I had been given to heal and have a normal life. It was the beginning of me meeting other Chubbys. Those men who used, humiliated and destroyed the child I was. After that time the little girl who, with her suntanned face, had called out, '*Hola*,' to her friends, spun round to the music at the *fiesta* and rushed excitedly into school full of stories about her holiday disappeared, leaving in her place a little girl who heard screams inside her head.

21

On the days when I did not go to my uncle, Kat and I would take our bicycles out and ride along the lanes until we reached the purple heather-covered moors. Sometimes we would spot a field devoid of animals and farm workers, rest our bikes against a hedge and climb over the gate.

There we would lie on our backs, our heads resting on our arms and the last of the autumn sun warming our faces. With my fists screwed up like binoculars, I held them to my eyes as I searched for wildlife but it was only common small brown birds that I was able to find in the curve of my fingers. I felt a tug of yearning for Spain, with its forests and peace, and wanted to see again the flight of a solitary eagle.

It was on one of those excursions that Kat told me how a woman got pregnant. I knew that she was in a dark mood when we had set out that morning. Her mouth was turned down at the corners, making her look sullen and tired, but it was not until we reached the moors that she told me what was wrong.

The moment she was off her bicycle and into the field, she flung herself on to the ground and looked morosely up at the sky. I waited for her to say something, but she sighed deeply and looked at me bleakly. 'Do you know what my mother's gone and done now?' she asked, rolling her eyes.

All I knew about Kat's mother was what Kat had told me about her, although she was very friendly when she saw me. Not having a clue as to what she might have done, I remained silent.

'She's gone and got herself pregnant. Pregnant at her age! She's having a bloody baby in five months. A little sister or brother for me – as if I want one. She told me this morning. It was as if she thought I should be pleased. She was all coy and soppy-eyed with his hands on her stomach all the time to feel it kicking. Ugh, how embarrassing is that?'

It was then that she informed me of how women got pregnant.

'How could she?' Kat exclaimed in disgust. 'It's gross.' I sat with my arms round my knees, listening to her rant on about how revolting the thought of what her mother and new husband did together was.

But as she spat out her hurt and frustration I felt a creeping sense of horror coming over me. 'Do you get pregnant every time you do that?' I asked tentatively.

Kat, wrapped up in her own problem, did not question why a little girl of eight wasn't shocked at the description of the sex act but curious about the results. 'I think so. Why else would they do it? It's so gross,' she said, with the positive conviction of a ten-year-old, sure she is right.

I pushed the sinking feeling that Kat's information had given me deep within the recesses of my mind for I did not want her to notice that anything was wrong. Instead I tried to console her, but nothing was going to make Kat feel like smiling that day.

'Got your Walkman with you?' she asked and, relieved

that I could do something for her, I brought it out of my duffel bag. She had brought her own headphones and tapes. 'Let's listen to these,' she said, 'not your baby stuff.' I bit back a retort on the injustice of that remark – hadn't I chosen ones by stars she said she liked? She slipped a tape in – and for the first time I heard a different type of music than anything that was listened to in my home. The first cassette was by a band called the Sex Pistols.

'It seriously pisses my mother off when she hears it,' Kat shouted at me over the music – we each had our headsets on. I did not ask her why she let her mother hear it when she had her own Walkman and could listen in silence. But I had already learnt by then that 'pissing off' her mother and stepfather was something she enjoyed. 'But they can't stop me listening to what I want – my dad buys them for me,' she said defiantly.

In that field, cigarettes dangling from the corners of our mouths, Coke bottles frothing over, we bobbed about, joined through each headset to the single body of the Walk-man. 'This is how you pogo,' she shouted, as she jumped straight up and down to the most controversial band of the decade. To us it came highly recommended by one factor alone: our parents had been outraged by it. Relishing the words that had shocked the older generation, we sang together Johnny Rotten's version of 'God Save The Queen'.

But as we danced and smoked, all I could think of was what Kat had told me. Babies might look very small to a full-grown person but to me they were quite big. Which meant that if one was growing inside me, might it not make my stomach burst open when it was ready to come out? I felt cold waves of fear at that thought.

For several days I fretted, and every morning I looked at my stomach to see if it had grown bigger. I was sure I felt something moving inside. Was it a baby kicking? I asked myself, in a panic. In the end, after several worried days, I decided to confront my mother.

'I think I'm going to have a baby,' I said baldly and, to my surprise, she did not react with the shocked response I was hoping for but dreading.

'Don't be silly, Jackie,' was all she said, without even looking up from the newspaper.

'I am,' I insisted, as my imagination took me from possible to definite.

The newspaper was lowered slowly and the look of resigned impatience I was now so used to was directed at me yet again. 'Whatever makes you think that?'

I swallowed hard, clenched my fists so that my nails made tiny marks on my palms. This time I was determined she would listen to me. Undeterred by the look she was giving me, I managed to blurt out that I knew how babies were made.

'Don't be silly, you're too young –'

'I do know!' I practically screamed at her. 'The man sticks his thing –'

There was a shout of outrage from my appalled mother. 'Stop this nonsense. Don't talk dirty, Jackie. I won't have it, not in this house. Ever. Do you hear me?' Then a hint of worry came into her voice. 'Who told you that? One of those children from that dreadful council estate, I suppose.' Although there were no council houses within our village boundaries, there were in the next village. A small percentage of the children who lived there had now started to attend our village school, something that my mother was far from happy with.

I knew better than to say it was Kat. I could just imagine my mother storming over to the neighbours' house and Kat refusing to speak to me ever again. And I would probably be banned from mixing with her. As my parents were reluctant to let me take my bicycle out on the roads without her, I thought it better to keep that information to myself. So I just nodded.

'Jackie, what are you trying to tell me?'

'I've done that,' I screamed, before bursting into tears.

'You disgusting little girl,' she started, and I closed my ears to what followed. I knew from the words being hurled at me that she didn't believe I had done much, but she knew I had been playing games in which parts of the body that should be kept out of view had been exposed.

Through her tirade I heard words I had heard time and again and would continue to hear for some years. How I was a disgrace, a constant embarrassment. On and on she went, until I wanted to place my hands over my ears. If I had hoped deep down that she would put her arms round me and ask what was really troubling me, I finally knew then that it was not going to happen. Out of fear, I had given myself an opening to tell her what was happening every weekend. But she made it clear she had no intention of hearing the words spoken silently between the lines of what I had said aloud. I looked at her then, her perfectly made-up face contorted with anger and disgust, and I knew I could never tell her. She would not believe me.

'I never want to hear you say anything like that again. We've had this conversation before, Jackie, haven't we? Just after Christmas, wasn't it?' and she was off again.

'I think you're just deliberately trying to shock and upset me,' she continued, 'and I don't know why you would want to do that.' She said it had been a waste of time taking me away. 'I told your father it was, but he insisted.' She added that there was nothing more she could do for me. She finished by forbidding me to mix with common children and finally dismissed my words entirely by calling me a stupid child and telling me that little girls under eleven could simply not get pregnant. She did not tell me why but, despite my despair, I was relieved that a baby was not going to burst out of my stomach.

Humiliated by her venom, I slunk to my room and sat there with my head in my hands, looking down at my feet. My fingers twisted the ends of my hair as I thought through the reality of my situation. I could never say anything to my parents. They didn't love me and they wouldn't believe me if I told them about my uncle and Chubby.

I felt as dirty as my mother had said I was. I went into the bathroom, undressed and then washed every part of my body with meticulous concentration. I soaped and scrubbed but the dirt, invisible to those who did not know it was there, remained.

Somewhere during that time, Florence disappeared from my life and my teddy bears became just children's toys. With that realization came sadness, for it was then that it dawned on me that I was really on my own.

22

My memories of the next few years are a kaleidoscope of jumbled pictures. Were there nice times? I think so, but any recollection of them is hidden under the layers of the times that happened next.

There was pain – pain inflicted on me by men who, too excited by acting out their fantasies and satisfying their need, forgot to be careful with my small body. Later, as I grew a little older, there were bruises from slaps and the marks of fingers that had pressed hard into soft flesh. Marks that I became skilled at hiding. 'I slipped'; 'I knocked myself'; 'My throat is sore so I need to cover it' were just some of the many excuses that I made to hide my shame. At school before PE classes I often had to pretend to have a cold. Shivering, my face burning with fear at undressing and those telltale marks being exposed for everyone to see, I stuttered out my excuses.

The anger grew. I gazed sullenly at my mother whenever she spoke, and left the room when my father was there. I couldn't bear to see the worry and disappointment that so often flitted across his face whenever his eyes rested on me.

At school, I became surly and uncommunicative. Art classes were the only lessons that interested me. But when the other children drew pictures in which the sun was always shining, I drew something quite different.

It was years after I had drawn them that I saw them again. For some reason my mother had kept them. She must have taken them out of my room after I'd left and, instead of throwing them out as I would have expected, had rolled them up neatly and saved them. Just holding them was enough to bring the old anger back. Sometimes there were just violent slashes of dark colours streaking across the page, at others furious squiggles where the paintbrush had been applied so heavily it had almost ripped the pages. There was one of a child with fat tears running down its face. But the most disturbing was the picture of a house under a black sky. There were no trees or flowers in pretty pastel shades as other children drew, just red and grey streaks, representing flames, bursting out of the roof. There were no figures standing outside it. When I had drawn that, was I really imagining everyone inside the house had been devoured by fire? When you looked closely, the small house in the corner was just a black square – yes, I mentioned that little house before and the person who lived there: my uncle.

As I held and examined it, I saw an image of a child small for her age, her face screwed up in concentration as she expressed her anger and hopelessness in the only way she knew how: by drawing them. Each time she put her brush or crayon on the paper the screams filled her head; screams that only she heard.

23

'We don't want you going to your aunt and uncle's so often,' said my mother.

'No,' added my father, as he lowered the paper and smiled at me. 'We miss you too much. We're going to do things as a family, just like we did in Spain.'

I thought about how, when I went to school, I heard other children talking about their weekends and holidays. Now I would be able to join in. I had never told the teachers that most weekends I was sent away, for I never wanted them to ask, 'What did you do there?'

'Tomorrow we'll take our bicycles and go into the country for a picnic,' they both said, almost in unison.

'You're more important than the hairdresser and my dinner parties or even Daddy's golf,' my mother added laughingly, as she gently stroked my hair off my face. They both smiled warmly at me as I basked in their love.

That evening she cooked my favourite supper and afterwards, instead of going to my room to watch videos on my own, we all sat down together and watched television. I sat next to my mother on the settee and rested against her. I could smell her light flowery perfume and she, feeling me pressed against her, smiled and put her arm round my shoulders to pull me even closer to her.

The next morning, no sooner had I come down the

stairs than the picnic basket was strapped to the back of my father's bicycle.

Other family groups were riding their bikes on the country roads that warm sunny day. Pink-faced with hard pedalling, little blond boys waved at us as we overtook them, and looking up at the clear blue sky, I saw the white vapour trails left by aeroplanes as they flew overhead.

We came to the fields where a lush green carpet thick with daisies and buttercups beckoned us. We dismounted and walked, our legs brushed by flowers. In the distance I saw rabbits, their retreating white tails bobbing as they disappeared into the long grass.

'This is the perfect place,' my mother said, as she spread out a brightly coloured woollen rug for us to sit on before opening the wicker basket. It contained soft drinks and an assortment of appetizing food.

She handed round sandwiches and we ate and drank. My mother picked buttercups and held them under my chin. 'To see if you like butter,' she told me solemnly. 'If you do there will be a small yellow circle there.'

'And do I?' I asked, giggling with the tickly feeling of her stroking them against my skin.

'Yes, you like butter, all right,' she declared, and we all laughed.

My parents lay basking in the sun and I picked daisies and made them into chains that I strung around my mother's ankles and wrists.

Later I dozed, my head resting in my mother's lap, her hand stroking my back.

We were tired when we returned home but not so tired that my mother refused to read me a story when I climbed into bed. I was nearly asleep by the time she had finished and I felt her lips brush my cheek before she left my room. 'Night-night, my darling,' she whispered, as she closed the door.

When morning came, I woke to a fuzzy feeling of happiness.

The memory of the previous day was sharp and clear. The picture of it replayed in my head while I came fully awake. It was then that I realized memory was unreliable: that day had never happened. During the night my imagination had painted a pastel picture of how I wished my life to be, a fantasy created by my subconscious that unleashed waves of longing – longing to be a normal little girl whose parents loved her and who took every measure to keep her safe.

My grief when I faced the reality of my life was expressed by a string of inarticulate words directed at Paddington who, in my unhappiness, I clutched tightly to me. My body shook with sobs of loss, followed by an open-mouth wail before I pressed my face hard against Paddington's furry body to deaden the sounds of my despair.

For what had really happened that weekend was that my aunt and uncle had told my mother at the last minute that they had to go away – something to do with my aunt's sister being unwell. When my mother told me that my weekend visit had been cancelled, I could tell by her clipped tone that she was more than annoyed.

'Well, Jackie,' she said, tight-lipped, 'that's really inconvenient. We're having a dinner party tonight and I don't want you creeping around. Do you understand?'

'Yes, I know,' I mumbled, feeling a surge of resentment against her.

That Saturday progressed as all the others did when I stayed at home for the weekend. My father left early to play golf and I accompanied my mother to the hairdresser and the shops. I was given an early supper and two videos were handed to me as I laid down my knife and fork. 'I got you these to keep you busy. Remember you're to stay in your room, Jackie,' my mother reiterated sternly.

'Why?' I asked, in the petulant, whiny tones of the aggrieved that I had learnt to perfect. They earned me, as I had expected, a stony stare followed by an exasperated sigh.

'Because I said so,' my mother replied and, knowing that no other explanation would come my way, I meekly agreed.

That night, remembering how I had been discovered the previous time, I waited until the music was turned up before I crept down the stairs.

The guests were dressed as cowboys and cowgirls. The women's fringed skirts were so short that they only just covered their knickers and the men were wearing chaps.

I watched through the half-open door as they danced and kissed people who were not their partners, but then, scared that I would be seen, I scuttled back up the stairs to my room.

This time, instead of feeling unsettled by what I had seen, I was just filled with anger. I hated them and concluded they must hate me too. This was why my mother never wanted me around. I knew that what they were up to involved the same sort of things my uncle made me do. Was this what the adult world was all about?

But I knew that other people's families were not like

mine. Even Kat, with all her complaints, had a mother who appeared to love her, and a father who spent time with her whenever he could. I had heard the excited Monday-morning buzz at school as each child chattered about what they had done at the weekend. Enviously I stood quietly by and listened to them talk about family outings to the cinema, going into the countryside for picnics and taking trips to the seaside.

That was the type of childhood I so desperately wanted.

I began to resent the other children in my class. I glowered when I heard them talking of things they had done and they, sensing my anger, avoided me more and more. Little groups of friends stopped their conversation when I approached, which fuelled my rage and resentment.

My fingers started to reach out and painfully nip those smug, contented children who were unaware I was standing near them. My feet tried to trip them up and my fists lashed out when the inner fury swelled so forcefully inside me that a teacher had to rush and restrain me.

As I grew bigger, my small hands were clenched into hard fists when I hit out indiscriminately and my kicking feet were strong enough to inflict pain. By the time I was ten some teachers refused to let me into their classes. 'Disruptive to the rest,' they started to say when, once again, I was made to spend my time outside the door. Underneath I sensed a growing fear of me and my wild actions.

There was one boy, however, who did not seem to be intimidated by my behaviour. His eyes would challenge me, his smirk mocked me and he would snigger as I walked past. 'Loopy Jackie,' he would hiss aggressively, so that only I could hear.

My glares had no effect on him and his bony fingers would reach out and pinch the soft places on my arms. His foot would trip me. When he did these things to me, I would hear the sniggers of the other children and see the teacher look down, determined not to interfere.

I knew that my classmates and those who tried to instil some knowledge and discipline into me thought it was time I was taught a lesson, which succeeded in enraging me even more. Over the weeks that followed, that boy became the person to whom I redirected all my pent-up anger with the world.

I waited until he, with the confidence of so many bullies, went too far. Not only did he hiss at me when he was giving out schoolbooks but he yanked hard on my plait when he was standing behind me. I saw the teacher, her blue eyes watching us, a slight smile on her face; a smile I had learnt to recognize in an adult – it showed that they derived pleasure from my discomfort. I knew that she had seen what he had done and decided to pretend she had not. I waited, biding my time, for I knew if I kept quiet, the boy would make a mistake. Later that day he did.

It was in the afternoon when he stood in the wrong place, positioned between the wide-open classroom door and the wall behind it. I felt the pressure in my head as I saw my opportunity. 'Now! Do it now, Jackie,' screamed the voice that lived inside me. I leapt forward, seized the handle and smashed the door as hard as I could into him so that he was crushed against the wall. I heard him scream, saw him fall and triumphantly stood there watching his fractured nose bleed as he writhed with pain.

The class was in an uproar. The teacher caught hold of

me, dragged me from the room and told me to stay outside while she dealt with the injured boy. Then it was back to the headmistress's study and, once again, my parents were summoned to be notified of my appalling behaviour.

'What made you do it?' the headmistress had asked. 'You could have hurt him even more than you did.'

But I could not explain to her that, as much as the boy's torments had angered me, it had been the sight of that smile on the teacher's face that had brought the rage to the surface.

I opened my mouth to try to tell her, but I could find no words, so I gave one of my indifferent shrugs that I had learnt infuriated the teaching staff, and looked expressionlessly at the floor.

That violent act led to another visit to the psychologist and another lecture about what a lucky little girl I was. His questions to me and my mother never once touched on what might have been at the root of the problem. I don't know what he wrote in his notes, maybe nothing much, as I have no copy of them in my file.

24

I only had two interests before I was twelve: my bicycle and listening to music. I found riding out of our village into the country reduced my anger, and music transported me to another place. Not for me the sweet, catchy harmonies of the boy bands and schmaltzy pop groups, such as Abba, that my classmates adored. I liked the more powerful voices of Annie Lennox, Debbie Harry and Siouxsie Sioux. When my black mood refused to lift, it was the loud thump of heavy rock and the anti-establishment lyrics of the punk bands that I wanted to listen to.

The music I had discovered might not have been the sort that other children of my age or even my parents liked, but I wanted sounds I could escape into, sounds that shared my anger and helped me find oblivion.

I would let my mind wander as I listened to the harsh, angry rock songs shouted out by young men whose lives were already being wrecked by drugs and alcohol. They bellowed out words that told of a bleak anarchistic future that some did not even live to see. They sang of lost dreams, of disillusionment, and as I listened to those lyrics, my mind was free and the world distant.

I pleaded with my parents for more and more music and, pleased that I had found an interest, they bought me whatever tapes I asked for.

In my room I watched an interview with Johnny Rotten on the TV. With spiky blond hair and wild eyes, he shocked the world with his swearing and disrespect for everyone and everything that people like my parents valued. I loved him. He was 'the man', I decided.

25

After that initial occasion, a family holiday in Spain was never mentioned again. I knew that my father still owned the *finca*, and sometimes I wanted to ask him if we could go again, but pride stopped me. I had overheard too many fragments of conversations not to know that my mother did not want to take me away with them.

Instead I spent half of my summer holiday with my uncle while my parents went to places like Italy and the South of France. I only knew that because I saw the glossy brochures that my mother left lying around.

Staying with my uncle was not just restricted to my parents' summer holidays and numerous weekends, but as my behaviour became more unpredictable, some of our short half-term breaks as well.

'Heaven knows, Jackie, why you can behave for him and not me,' my mother said repeatedly, while my father said little and just looked at me with the puzzled, worried expression I had grown to hate. My weak protests that I wanted to spend time with Kat were ignored. 'You can see her during the week or next weekend. We're having a party this Saturday,' was always the abrupt answer.

Was my uncle scared that as I grew older and more troubled I might also become less malleable? Was it fear that made him arrange what was to happen next? Or was it that his clients were demanding more? I don't know,

I never asked him, and, of course, it's too late now. But I do know they were customers, not friends. Over those years, not only had he been able to use me as his toy he had also been able to make money from me. I had come to understand that quite young. The drink and drugs I had been given had not blurred my senses completely, and I had seen the wads of banknotes handed to him by sweaty-palmed men anxious to get their hands on what they had paid for.

Whatever the reasons, he decided to move my degradation up a notch or two.

There had been times, indeed many times, when my uncle was present while one of his 'friends' had sex with me. Sometimes he was behind the camera and sometimes he just watched. By then, of course, I had learnt to float out of my body and look down at the child, who lay there passively, drowsy from whatever she had been given. After it was over, I was furious with that little girl. Why did she never refuse to do as her uncle told her? Her submission over the years had turned her into a mute supplicant to his controlling Svengali.

There was always the bright light, which caused her uncle and the camera to merge and become one menacing, misshapen shadow, and the men who twisted her body into whatever position they wanted before forcing that thing into either her mouth or between her legs. And all the time she lay there silently, not protesting. Of course I could feel it inside me, but I was separate from what was taking place.

There were the men who eagerly swapped places and took their turn behind the camera, snapping photos. Then it was their chance to be the observer, the one who watched through the blinking eye of the lens. Some of them I grew to recognize, for they visited several times; others came once, then disappeared. I would like to think that perhaps my body had reminded them too much of a loved daughter or grandchild, and shame had driven them away. But in fact I believe they moved on to pastures new.

Then there were the occasions when, with a new device my uncle had purchased, the camera could be operated remotely and closer to where I was lying. That was when he was asked to join in, which he rarely refused to do.

It was a few months after my eleventh birthday that my periods started and my body began to change. My uncle began to lose interest. However, my new shape had the opposite effect on some of his 'friends'. They came to his house when his wife was at work, men I had not seen before.

There were the ones whose guilty eyes avoided mine. They did what they did, finished quickly with me, said little, dressed hurriedly, and left. While some leered at my nakedness. And then there were the others, hard-faced men who handed over the cash and demanded speedy delivery from my uncle's darkroom, stating that they had clients waiting for the latest pictures.

Sometimes they were finished within a few minutes, but however long they took, they were never in that room longer than an hour. But I talk as though their pleasure only lasted while they were there. The photographs extended it for days or even weeks, until the men came back for more.

It was those pictures, hidden in dark, secret places, of

themselves or another man abusing a child, which enabled them to play out their fantasies or relive that illicit time. It was the thought of those men relishing every detail in private, as much as what they had done to me, that caused my worst nightmares. Looking at those sordid pictures, they could again feel the excitement of being completely in control and of wielding their power over a person too small to fight back. Instead that child could only turn a frightened face to their tormentor: they knew there was no escape and no one to turn to.

I learnt over the time I spent with my uncle that the men who molest children fall into two categories. Some have the arrogant belief that the children, however much they deny it, like what is being done to them. They watch a small crumpled form crying, hear the protests and the whimpers, yet still they want to believe that three-, four-, five-, six- and seven-year-olds have dormant sexual feelings hidden in their defenceless bodies. When those men look in the mirror, the reflection they see is not of an evil man, but of a man who loves children and whom children love. That man manipulates his victims by brainwashing them into believing that what has been done to them was partly of their own making. It is never 'my' secret when he tells the child to be quiet, but 'ours'. Never him who would get into trouble, but 'we'. He plays on a child's emotions and gains acquiescence with barely disguised threats and reassurances of love. My uncle was such a man.

The second type sees children as having been put into the world purely for his pleasure. With crafty, calculating knowledge, he understands that a child who is merely made to feel pain might talk. But when the humiliation is so complete, a small child's agony is overridden by shame. Then that man knows the child never will say anything.

The Chubbys of this world belonged to the second type and, at eleven, I was to meet the worst of them.

There had been occasions when two men had performed sexual acts on me at the same time, and there had been times when pain was inflicted clumsily. But as my body started to develop, my uncle decided to add another dimension to what he would allow.

This time, a group of four men rang the bell. Earlier he had turned the settee into a bed that dominated the workroom so I knew he was expecting company. He had given me the drink that made everything hazy before he led them into the room. I could hear them talking in the hall, rough, deep male voices that sounded more businesslike than excited.

As they entered I made that part of myself, the part of me that they could never touch, leave my body. Almost devoid of feeling, I rested somewhere above them, watching as they spoke to the young girl sitting on the bed. I could not make out the words and when they did not receive a reply, they ordered her to remove her clothes. She swayed slightly as she stood up and undressed, but no gentle hand steadied her. That group just watched through narrowed eyes.

I could see her long plait hanging down her back, her slight shoulders hunched, the beginning of tiny breasts, still not large enough for a teenage bra but showing all the same, and a white, white face wiped clean of any trace of animation or even apparent awareness of what was happening to her.

She laid her jeans and T-shirt over a stool, then sat

down again on the bed-settee, where she thought they wanted her.

'Not there,' said one. 'Move, girl.' He pointed with a nicotine-stained finger to a hard wooden chair. Dazed, she looked at him, as though the words made little sense. With an impatient snort he yanked her to her feet and sat her down by pushing her shoulders hard so that the bottom of her spine crashed against the seat. Before she could realize what was happening, another man had pulled her arms back and tied them behind her. Her head flopped to one side with dizziness as the men circled their captive. She was not fully developed, that girl, but already her waist tapered above her small sharp hip bones and her skin stretched tautly across her stomach. I could see a faint shadow between her legs, proclaiming that her body was changing from child to woman as, wraithlike and invisible to them, I watched those men and observed from above what they did to her.

Large rough hands stroked those small budding breasts, then one squeezed her nipple hard. The sudden pain made her body twitch and a faint groan escaped from her pale lips. They smiled then, gloating, leering smiles.

They took out bulldog clips, the big ones used for keeping piles of paper tidy, placed them on those tiny breasts and, forcing her legs apart, somewhere between her legs. I knew they were hurting her for I also felt a sharp stabbing pain shoot through my body, as though in sympathy with what she was enduring. Her eyes closed, but behind her lids I saw them fluttering.

They had oral sex with her. With as much care as a man urinating, they unzipped their trousers, held her head and jerked their fluids into her mouth, but still she did not stir. Then, bored with her passivity, they wanted something else.

They untied her, threw her on the bed and climbed on top of her.

Two of them could not get a second erection and, watching, I breathed a sigh of relief, for those men were big. I thought then that if all of them stuck those purple engorged things in her they might damage her small frame beyond repair. It was the third, who I saw had become rock hard, who suddenly flipped her over, spread her slender child-legs wide, then entered her.

I think I lost consciousness then. I felt that unimaginable pain going through her body and I knew flecks of blood were spotting the tops of her legs. I saw her struggle to regain awareness, but her eyes as they flickered open were dull from whatever had been given to her. She watched as the men zipped themselves up and straightened their clothes and she saw the thick wad of money passed to her uncle.

I felt no pity for the girl and the pain I knew she was suffering. Instead it was anger that coursed through me; anger not at the men or even the man who had once professed to love her, but at the girl and her acquiescence. How could she have just accepted what had happened without putting up any resistance?

She was calling me back to re-enter her body; the body that was so dirty, so defiled. I wanted to stay where I was, in the air, looking down, but a stronger force compelled me to return.

That was nearly the end of the first part of my story, the one I waited more than twenty years to tell.

26

'It wasn't then,' I said to the woman sitting quietly opposite me. 'It should have been, but it wasn't then that my uncle lost me, lost his control over me. It was a few weeks later.'

'Take your time, Jackie. When you're ready, tell me what happened next,' said the sympathetic voice of the person from whom I had been seeking help.

I paused, for it was that part more than any other that still fills me with shame and had finally driven me to seek professional help. I needed the movie in my head to stop. It played continuously, on a loop. The characters were the child, my teenage self and many others. The therapist waited patiently, as she always did, for me to continue, understanding what it must have cost to reveal that part of me.

'That was the day I met the man,' I said haltingly, my voice barely a whisper. 'The one my uncle was afraid of. He had a whip. He wanted to lash me with it, I knew that. But it was the other strap he carried that frightened me even more, for that was the one he would tie round my neck. The one he would pull tighter and tighter to cut off my air while he had sex with me. In the photos it would look as though I was dying, and I was scared then that I might. Might die, I mean.'

Years had passed since that day, but my body still shook

at the memory and my voice dropped until I was mumbling so quietly that, even leaning forward, she struggled to hear me. I felt the old shame again, not the emotion where heat flushing through the body sends a telltale crimson wave to stain the face, but a blackness I wanted to disappear into. Not wishing to meet her eyes, I averted my head, but she wasn't going to allow me to avoid her.

'And then, Jackie? Tell me what happened then,' she said, more urgently, perhaps sensing a breakthrough in my therapy.

I gulped, dug my nails into my hands and, for the first time, I was able to blurt out what I had wanted to say for so long.

'I climbed off that bed,' I said, in a loud, determined voice, 'grabbed the whip, tore it out of his hands. Yes, I stopped him. And then – then I just walked out of the room.'

'Very good, Jackie,' she said, and smiled warmly at me. 'You're progressing.'

It was two years since I had started therapy. Two years in which, gradually, my life had, like a huge tangle of knotted string, been unwound, strand by strand, and examined. Over that time I had begun to cover each scene in the film of my past with a new one: one in which I was the winner.

It was only when that was done that I had the power to look again at the truth and deal with it.

It was when I came to understand that the memories of my past had become too much for me to carry any longer that I had decided to seek out a therapist. I was an adult, and I looked for the right person as selectively as another woman might have looked for a lover.

When I finally found her she did not try to allay my fears that she would be the same as the others I had met. Instead she said, 'Let's just take it one session at a time, Jackie,' and I had agreed. Each week I turned up and revealed to her, piece by piece, those parts of my life that I had been unable to deal with.

To begin with there were times when I could tell her no more than what could be contained in a few short sentences. When you have been so down, so destroyed, you are careful. Talk, yes, that's allowed, but always with a little bit held back. The little bit that might just expose the real person hiding behind the mask. It takes both time and courage to allow all defences to be stripped away until what is left behind is just a vulnerable, needy person. The therapist, understanding that, had made no demands. She just waited for me to trust her enough to allow her to help.

It had taken nearly a hundred visits before I could tell her the new version of what happened when I met the man with the whip.

By then she had learnt nearly everything there was to know about me. Every week she had sat calmly in her chair while I stumbled over the randomly selected sections of my story that I felt I could talk about that day.

Her questions were always small ones, for it was me who had to talk, not her, and me who had to come to my own conclusions. Her job was only to lead me to the place where I could do that.

But I knew that there were parts of my story that she couldn't leave in her file when she went home: the parts that had moved her. It was then that she would fire an unexpected question, and her eyes betrayed the compassion behind her professionalism.

She knew without me telling her again what had really happened on the day I broke free from my uncle, for I had already told her.

27

It was when he brought the whip man round, the man he was scared of, that my ties with my uncle were finally severed.

What was so frightening about that man? I don't know. It was just that, on seeing him, my legs turned to jelly and my body shook. There was nothing outstanding about how he looked. He was of average height and average appearance. He was a nondescript man – if I had passed him in the street, he would have gone unnoticed.

Maybe it was his aura of coldness. With him there was not even a hint that he was in that room for anything other than the reason he gave. But even that seemed different: there was no furtive excitement about him. He handed my uncle money, not discreetly as the others did, so I wouldn't see it, but as though I was of no importance at all. 'Get undressed,' he ordered.

I reached for the glass, the drink that made everything blur.

He knocked it out of my hand. 'You won't need that,' he said. 'Now clean it up.' Without looking at him, I fetched a cloth, knelt and did as he'd ordered.

I heard my uncle say something.

'Don't want pictures of a zombie, now, do we? Like the last ones you sent me. They don't sell to my people. She's old enough – time she enjoyed it anyhow.'

He looked at me then. I was standing, clutching the cloth, uncertain what to do next. 'Let's have a look at the goods, then,' he said. 'I told you to get your clothes off, girl, so do it.'

Looking into his face, terror overcame any other feelings. Under his cold gaze, I stepped out of my jeans, pulled my skimpy jumper over my head and stood there in my cotton pants. His hand gestured impatiently for me to remove them.

'Now you,' he said to my uncle, having stripped himself. And that was when I saw the first signs of fear on my uncle's face. He might have joined in before, but this was different. This time another man was giving the orders.

'We're going to make a nice little movie here,' he said. 'You're good in them, aren't you, Jackie?'

He told my uncle to lie on the floor.

'Now, Jackie, open your mouth wide.'

Knowing what was expected of me, I obeyed. It was as I lowered my head towards my uncle's flaccid penis that I felt the leather belt go round my neck.

'I've got another one, girlie,' he told me, and a searing pain went through me as the second belt swished down. 'Now,' he said, 'each time you stop you get this. Understand?'

I did.

He entered me then. His nails dug into my legs as he pushed himself roughly into me. This time was different: without the drink that dulled my senses I could not leave my body. No, this time it was me who felt the pain and me who gasped with it. The leash tightened and the whip came down harder. 'Told you what would happen if you stopped,' he said.

There was blackness in front of my eyes.

'It feels like dying, doesn't it, Jackie? Well, I'm not going to let you die too fast.'

Another pain shot through me from his thrusts and the belt tightening on my neck.

I heard his voice asking me over and over, 'Don't you want to know what it feels like to die, Jackie?' Each time I gasped the whip descended. I thought every time was the last because he moved his body slightly away from me. But I was wrong: it was just so there was enough bare flesh available for him to mark. I heard my uncle protest. His voice was shaking with fright for I think he believed then that the man was capable of killing me. But while that thought might have terrified him, all I wished was that it would happen.

When he had finished, I lay on that mattress in too much pain to move. It was the man who rolled me over. My uncle was sitting with a look of horror on his face, too scared to move or speak.

'Hey, Jackie,' the man said, and jerked hard on my hair.

I looked up into his face again.

He grinned at me. Then he stood up, put his foot on my chest and pissed on me. Holding that thing in his hand, he aimed it towards my face, and before I could move, a stream of hot yellow liquid rained down on me. I shut my eyes tight, trying to block out what was happening. It was warm and sticky, and I felt it running down my neck and into my hair.

I didn't look at my uncle when the man left. I could hear him crying but I didn't look at him. Instead I got up and walked on unsteady feet to the bathroom. I poured in bubble bath and ran the taps until the bath was almost full and the room was full of steam. Then I climbed in. I submerged myself in the hot suds, washed my hair and let it float around me. Then I soaped my body, scrubbed every bit of it, even the places that were sore. I could smell him, the rank stench of sweat and the other nameless fluids that had been smeared on my body. I let the water out, then refilled the bath.

I lay there for a long time. I could see the slight ripples as the water moved in time to my heartbeat, but that was all. It cooled around me but still I did not move. All I could think was that if I let my head go under the water I would die. I tried: I closed my eyes, sank under the surface, but then I found I couldn't. The will to live betrayed me; it was stronger than I had believed.

I cried then, fat tears that rolled down my face in a silent torrent until I thought there could be no more moisture left in me. That was the last time I cried. That was the day my tears dried up. Not one, either of happiness or sorrow, has run down my face since then. Oh, there have been many times when I have wanted them but the comfort of tears has deserted me.

Instead I found comfort in pain. Razors became my secret friends. Droplets of blood that leaked from those little slashes high on my legs – my tears. Then the burns: candle wax was the best. The wheals it raised stung all day but left no lingering marks. And hadn't so many men shown me how that was done, dribbling wax first over their chests, then mine? They were wrong when they said I would come to enjoy it. I came only to endure it, but they had taught me one thing: that the longer pain lasts, the longer the escape from reality.

That day was my first lesson in inflicting physical pain upon my body to anaesthetize mental anguish. When I was dry I picked up a candle and lit it. Then I dribbled the hot wax over my chest. This time there were no men watching with their lecherous stares, no drooling mouths or excited, greedy eyes. This time it was only me I was doing it for. Only me.

Concentrate, I told myself, and gradually it worked. As the burning became the only thing I could feel, so the grip of the memories that had been eating into my mind weakened.

With that pain the string of my uncle's control was finally severed.

My focus shifted and I no longer saw the man who had exercised his power over me for so long. Instead I saw a weak, greedy man.

When I walked down the stairs to face him I felt contempt – pure contempt. With it came my freedom: freedom from him ever touching me again. I was not to know that although I was free of his control it would be many years before I could escape from the damage he had done.

'How old were you then?' my therapist had asked, the first time I had told her that part of my story.

'I was twelve,' I replied.

28

She had thrown questions at me then about what had happened next, for she knew from my medical records that my story had not ended there; that I had not just walked away and returned to normality.

'I stopped being a child,' I replied.

My aunt was told I had a sore throat because it was two days before I could talk. A scarf covered my bruises and my eyes burnt into my uncle's head as they followed him.

'Are you in hell?' were the first words I spoke to him when I had recovered my voice. 'I hope you are.'

Knowing he had lost me, he drew away.

I threw other words at him – 'pictures', 'police' and 'prison' – and for a while he believed me. I demanded money for my silence.

'Fuck you,' I said. 'Not such a big man now, are you?' I felt satisfaction at the expression on his face, where fear mingled with defeat. 'I want twenty pounds,' I said. 'I've earned it.' Those words betrayed, if nothing else did, that I was still a child for to me that was a vast sum. To him, it was a negligible amount of what he must have earned from me.

Without protest he went to a drawer and took out a roll of notes.

I believed as I took it that that was the start of my

rebirth. But, of course, that was not what it was: it was a further descent into misery.

I was just a child alone in the dark who, never knowing happiness, was now determined to be bad.

29

She had made no comment when I had told her that part. Instead she asked me about something quite different – or maybe in a way it was not. 'Were you never able to talk to one of the psychologists you saw?' she asked.

An image came into my head then of a small, dark-haired woman, who had looked at me kindly. I felt, the day I met her, that she saw me. Not the child with a file full of notes about her bad behaviour, but me.

'There was one,' I told her. 'I was about ten, perhaps a little younger but not much.'

She had insisted she wanted to talk to me on my own; that my mother could drop me off for that hour's session. When I went into her room she told me to take a seat next to her. With its armchairs and soft lighting thrown by several small lamps, it felt more like a sitting room than a doctor's office. I almost felt as though I was visiting her in her home. She told me her name but I can't remember what it was.

'You don't seem a happy little girl, Jackie,' was nearly the first thing that she said. That was when I thought she saw me. Really saw me, not the child described within the pages of a brown folder, the one who behaved badly. She looked so kind that just for a moment I wanted to go to her, climb on to her lap, tuck my head under her chin and feel the comfort of arms holding me.

I paused then and my therapist waited for me to continue.

'I couldn't bear to meet her eyes,' I said, as I remembered that day and the woman waiting patiently for me to speak. 'So I did what children do when an adult is about to ask them a question they don't want to answer. I ducked my head, crossed my arms and rested my hands on my shoulders.

'"I'm all right," was all I had said then, and I knew she didn't believe me.

'She asked me if there was anything I wanted to talk to her about, anything I wanted to share with her. But that fleeting moment when maybe I could have confided in her had gone.

'I had passed the six-year barrier by then,' I said ruefully. For a moment a look of puzzlement flitted across my therapist's face before it was followed by understanding, mixed with compassion.

It is those moments when our eyes meet that we are just two women in a room. One with a sad story she needs to tell the other, who is both moved and appalled by what she is hearing. Then the professional's mask slips back on before a crack appears in the wall that separates patient from therapist. It is important that both women remember their roles and why they are together. Sometimes it is not easy for me to remember that. After all, until just a short time ago it was only my therapist who had ever really got to know me, who had listened to me telling her of my secrets and my fear to which not even my closest friend was privy.

'The six-year barrier,' she said, with a sigh.

As both of us knew, that was an expression used by social services and psychologists about children who have been in long-term care. It is said and no doubt has been proved that, after six years in the system, the damage is done.

Like me, they will insist they are all right when asked. It is tactfully suggested to couples wanting to adopt an older child that first they try fostering. After all, should that arrangement not work, the child can be returned. But to hand back an adopted child would be, to say the least, frowned upon. So, in foster care they were shunted around from home to home. Some, of course, are lucky, but many are not.

Damaged children who see the adult world as having betrayed them often become incapable of accepting kindness. Deep down, they may want to but when it is offered it is often met with aggression. By the time I met the psychologist with kind eyes I had been sexually abused for more than six years. I would never willingly have taken a hand held out to help me.

'She was the first one I had liked so she was the one I had to get rid of.

'I played up all week, said I didn't like her and didn't want to see her again,' I told my therapist.

'And?'

'I didn't.'

There was nothing to add to that. There was not even a report in the file with her name on it.

30

Of course, my uncle, over the following weeks, asked for my forgiveness with tears in his eyes. 'I love you so much,' he blubbered. 'You know I do.'

'Wanker,' I said, pleased that at least I had some new words in my vocabulary to unleash on him.

'Jackie, I swear to you, I will never let those men in again.' Then, over and over again, he told me how much he cared for me, his eyes pleading with me to believe him.

When that got no more response from me than a disgusted and disbelieving look, he changed tactic. The thinning of the lips and the narrowing of the eyes altered his expression. I watched it change from pathetic and miserable, to sour and defensive.

'It was your fault as well, you know, Jackie,' he said, and a spiteful tone entered his voice. 'It's the sort of girl you are. Yes, that's what it was.'

I noticed it had transformed again, this time to the hectoring tone of self-righteousness. Something inside me, something I should have recognized as pride, told me to go, not to listen and just leave that place. But his voice held me there, just for a few seconds longer.

'You're no little innocent, Jackie. Men can see that you know what it's all about.'

I wasn't going to argue with him but I couldn't stop myself at least responding to his taunts. 'You fucking wanker,' I said, just in case he hadn't heard me the first time. 'Anyhow, I'm out of here. I'm going shopping. Oh, and, Uncle . . .' He looked up at me through red-rimmed eyes. The glimmer of hope in them faded at my next words. 'Better get yourself tidied up ready for Auntie, hadn't you?'

He made an effort to gather himself together and feebly offered to drive me to wherever I wanted to go.

'What? And be on my own with you for a moment longer? I don't think so,' I said derisively. 'Don't worry, I can get a bus.'

'Wait a minute, Jackie.'

I watched as he fumbled around in the drawer before pulling out two more ten-pound notes to add to the money I had demanded from him. Holding them out to me, he attempted to get round me again. 'Buy yourself something pretty while you're there.'

I snatched them out of his fingers and pushed them into the pocket of my shirt without any show of the gratitude he might have expected or even a word of thanks. 'Something pretty' were the last words I would have used to describe what I was planning to buy. Without giving him another glance, I slammed the door behind me and set off for town.

First I went to the local branch of a large chemist where I browsed the makeup section. Watching my mother shop had taught me the rudimentary facts about what I needed. I inspected the rows of powders, blushers, lipsticks and other items, all promising instant transformation. Samples covered the backs of my hands until I found a foundation that matched my skin tone, and an orange lipstick that

I thought was the perfect shade. Next, I chose a dark eye shadow, black liner and matching mascara. Then, from another aisle, I added red hair dye to my growing basket of purchases.

The next stop was the hairdresser. 'Cut it all off,' I said, flicking my plait in front of the stylist, a middle-aged woman, who viewed me worriedly.

'Are you sure, dear?' she asked, no doubt fearing that an avenging mother might appear, demanding that it was all put back together again.

'Yes,' I answered firmly. Then, because she still looked apprehensive, I continued, 'My mum's paying for it. It's a birthday present. I just became a teenager.' On the spur of the moment I added, 'And she's agreed I can start looking like one.' I gave her what I thought was my most winning smile.

It worked, and an answering one lit her face. 'Well, how nice. Shall we wash it first, dear?'

Not wanting to ask her how much extra that would cost, I just said, 'No, I did it myself this morning.' After all, I knew that, once I was back in my uncle's house, it was going to get wet enough. She beckoned me to take a seat in front of a large mirror. A voluminous black gown was draped around my shoulders. My plait was undone, my blonde hair brushed out so it fell in waves down my back. She picked up the scissors with her left hand and my mass of hair with her right. I felt cool air on my neck and heard the clipping sound as she snipped away, section by section, the hair my uncle had loved until a golden carpet lay on the floor.

I had not wanted it cut off in one piece – I knew from

my mother's friends that human hair was made into the hairpieces that so often adorned the coiffured heads of someone with less abundant hair than I had. I had no intention of allowing a part of me to be turned into a mass of curls that would spend the rest of its life sitting either on top of a nest of hair tinted the same golden shade as mine or pinned to a white plaster model. First I made her cut it halfway. Then, assessing the length, I twisted my head round and asked for a little more to come off until it hung a couple of inches above my shoulders.

I watched the junior sweep it up until it overflowed from the dustpan, then enjoyed seeing all those long strands thrown into a bin. That's the end of that, I thought.

A different face from the one I was used to stared back at me in the mirror. It seemed less round and my eyes appeared larger, but there was still the dusting of freckles across my nose that made my face look childlike. My fair brows and lashes were insignificant, but I already had plans to change them as well.

I ran my fingers through my hair, fluffed it so that soft curls fell around my face. Then, with hooked thumbs, I pulled it back behind my ears. 'Like it?' the hairdresser asked, as she held up a mirror for me to admire the back, and I nodded that I did.

Next stop was a small boutique that catered for teens. Inside I flicked through the rails in a determined fashion. Black jeans, a tight, long-sleeved T-shirt and a leather belt with a large silver buckle were soon piled on the counter. The assistant, a girl of around sixteen with black dyed hair and a silver stud in her nose, looked at me disdainfully. She pointedly moved the price tags so I was looking at them. 'It's my birthday today,' I improvised again. 'I'm thirteen,' I told her, in case she thought the clothes I had chosen were unsuitable for a twelve-year-old. 'My mother said I was old enough to choose for myself.' Another doubtful look came my way. 'It was her who told me about this shop,' I added ingratiatingly.

That was not exactly true – my mother never shopped in the area where my uncle lived. But when I had accompanied her to the hairdresser and glanced longingly at a similar shop's windows, she had said that the clothes were cheap and tacky. However, that was not the message I wanted to put across at this particular moment.

'Birthday' worked on her as it had on the hairdresser. The disdain left her face as she smiled and told me she remembered her first 'grown-up' outfit when it was her choice and not her mother's.

Seeing that she was now firmly on my side, I told her there was something else I wanted. Suddenly feeling shy, I said, 'A black bra, please.'

I didn't want to wear the sensible white teen one my mother had bought for me under duress beneath all my new black clothes.

A tape measure was wound expertly under my small breasts, then again in the centre. 'A size thirty, A cup,' she said. Seeing my pout of disappointment, she assured me that the bra I held was cleverly constructed to make the most of my measurement.

'OK,' I said. 'I'll take it – but I want to try everything on.' I gathered up my selection and went into the changing room. Off came the pleated skirt, the blouse with the Peter Pan collar and the pastel jumper that were the foundation of the wardrobe my mother considered suitable for a twelve-year-old girl. I put the bra on first. The shop assistant was right: I had a bust – a small one, but it was there all the same. Next I pulled on the jeans and T-shirt and buckled the belt round my waist.

'Yup,' I said to myself, as I preened in front of the mirror. Not quite there yet, but very cool.

'I'll take everything,' I said to the assistant. 'Birthday money,' I told her, as she caught sight of the notes I unfolded.

'Lucky girl,' she said.

Yeah, right, really lucky.

Out of the shop I went, clutching bags with the shop's smart logo on them. Then I walked round the corner to a shoe shop. No way was I going to wear my Clarks sandals with black jeans.

A pair of Dr Martens was what I wanted – those work boots with their thick soles and round toes that laced right up the ankle. It might have been the latest craze with teenagers but it was a style my mother called 'ugly'. I was determined to possess a pair.

'Birthday present,' I said, for the third time that day. Once again it worked, turning dour assistant into instant friend, and my latest purchase was placed in a bag.

All that shopping and spending was thirsty work, I decided, so I took myself to the popular local café. There I ordered a large frothy coffee. I spooned in the sugar and watched it sink slowly into the foam. I was pleased with my day's shopping, and for a few moments, I happily visualized returning to my uncle's and trying everything on together.

I pushed aside the thought that was lurking at the back of my mind: And then what?

Suddenly I became aware of the people around me and realized I was the only person sitting alone. At some tables groups of friends squeezed together, gesticulating and talking animatedly. There were couples, some with small children. On one adjacent table a mother sat with her teenage daughter. They looked happy in each other's company and were talking together, the girl giggling as her mother shared an amusing anecdote. All around me I could hear the buzz of laughter and chatter. I did not want to admit it to myself, but suddenly I felt an overwhelming sense of loneliness. It was as though I was in an invisible bubble that separated me from the world around me. It was as though I could see all those people but they were completely unaware of me.

A memory slid into my mind then. I had a picture of a pavement café with just a few tables and chairs outside a bakery. There, the air was scented with the aroma of freshly baked bread, coffee and pine trees. Above me the sky was a vast expanse of cloudless blue, and the huge yellow globe of the sun cast down its hot rays.

There was an olive-skinned man who spoke in a different language and placed in front of me a small glass of coffee. My father and I were sitting there together. He was smiling – a warm smile that felt like an embrace. He had bought me my first cup of coffee. Not like the frothy one with a scattering of cocoa powder on top that I was drinking now, just a freshly made brew of strong black coffee. I remembered the happiness I had experienced then, and recalled how content I had been simply to sit and bask in his company. I had thought it the most delicious thing I had ever tasted.

We had laughed together at a tabby cat that was sitting with its leg raised, slowly and carefully washing itself. 'Playing the cello,' my father had said, with a chuckle, and I laughed with him. But the memory failed to warm me. Instead it made me feel empty and sad. I pushed it firmly away: I didn't want any dark clouds hovering on the horizon to spoil this momentous day. 'I'm celebrating my independence,' I told myself, and picked up my cappuccino.

I dawdled in town a while longer and went to a music shop. I chose two cassettes, Madonna's *Like A Virgin*, and a hip-hop one the assistant recommended by some young black Americans called Run DMC. I cheered myself up with the thought that Kat would like listening to those and that my parents would hate them.

Shopped and now completely spent out, I made my way back to my uncle's house. I gave him what I hoped was a scornful look when he gasped at the sight of my shorn hair, then carried my bags upstairs and locked myself into the bathroom. I squeezed the tube of red dye on to my hair, rubbed it in to spread it evenly, then combed it through. Not wanting to splatter the bathroom's white tiles with red blotches, I decided that the safest place to sit while it 'took' was in the bath. I filled it, climbed in and waited for thirty minutes as the leaflet had instructed.

Once my watch told me the time was up, I ducked my head under the water, until I was reasonably sure I had rinsed it all off. Out of the bath, I blew it dry with my aunt's hair-drier. When I surveyed the finished job I thought that, although it was a bit patchy in places, it still looked pretty startling and that was exactly what I wanted.

Next it was time for my face to get its makeover. I smoothed on pale foundation to hide those freckles. Next I stroked mascara on to the blonde lashes I disliked so much. I had watched my mother 'put on her face' too often not to get it right, and leant in to the mirror to colour my eyebrows.

Then it was time for the final dramatic touch: the orange lipstick. One sweep and a new me stared back from the mirror. Enormous blue eyes, framed by thick black lashes, under a delicate arch of darkened brows, stared back at me. I felt a twinge of excitement – I looked so different. No longer was that childish plait swinging across my back but bright red hair curled around my face while a fringe swept across my forehead.

I wriggled into my new clothes and stood in front of the mirror. '*Voilà*,' I said out loud (well, I had attended *some* French classes). Goodbye to wearing children's clothes and looking like a child. The girl reflected in my aunt's bevelled mirror no longer looked like one who came from an expensive privileged suburb but one who was sussed and well able to take care of herself. And she certainly looked older than her twelve years. 'Wicked,' I said to myself. This was definitely the new me.

That day I felt as though I had been reborn. I stared into the glass willing the other child, the one who had been scared, controlled and needy, to leave. I was now a teenager who dressed in black clothes and wore orange lipstick. I looked like a person in charge of her life. 'One who won't take shit off anyone' were the words that came into my head.

The blue-eyed-blonde-haired-baby look that I so hated, and my uncle and his friends so loved, was gone. My darkened lashes looked longer, my face thinner. I placed one hand on my hip and tossed my hair. 'Wicked,' I said again. I flicked my hair one last time and sauntered nonchalantly downstairs to face my aunt and uncle.

They looked a bit startled. My uncle muttered something about me looking nice, and my aunt did as she normally did: cooked and made small-talk. 'You look very grown-up, dear,' was all she said.

When I returned home, my mother thought otherwise. No doubt fearing her wrath, my uncle had dropped me off with my case. Before I even had the front door open, he had sped away down the road.

A stream of questions was fired at me: where had the clothes come from, what had I done to my hair and what did I think I looked like? She wanted the red dye washed out immediately.

'Can't. It's semi-permanent,' I said defiantly. One or two washes might make it fade but that was all. She was only too aware of that.

'Whatever will the school say?' she moaned. 'Thank goodness it's the holidays and there's another week left. I'll ask my stylist what we can do with it.'

I didn't care what my teachers were going to think or what my mother thought. If the school hadn't thrown me out already, a few red curls were hardly going to make them.

So, ignoring her tirade, I just said it was my birthday

present. After all, I pointed out sarcastically, I was too old for teddy bears.

'But it's not your birthday, Jackie,' she said.

'Oh, well, Uncle said I could have my present early.' I gave one of the shrugs that infuriated her.

Another torrent of words poured out, this time claiming I was a spoilt child who could twist my uncle round my little finger. Finally she said she was going to talk to him and 'stop all this grown-up nonsense'. Little did she know that the last thing my uncle wanted was for me to be grown-up.

Well, he might as well take the blame for something, I thought, trying to keep the smirk off my face.

She, sensing truculence in me, objected again.

'Oh, get used to it,' I snarled eventually. 'Everyone looks like this.' A statement that both she and I knew was blatantly untrue, certainly not in the area where we lived.

Another frosty look came my way. 'Well, you're not going out looking like that. You're grounded.'

Our eyes met in anger, then hers dropped. 'I don't know what your father will say,' was her parting shot.

The argument was over. My father was not going to say much. He wanted a quiet life.

In my room I painted my nails black before I rang Kat to invite myself over. Then, with another coat of mascara and a renewed smear of lipstick, I left the house stealthily by the kitchen door, clutching the new cassettes. There was a limit, I thought, as to how much I could get away with.

When she saw my transformation, Kat looked more alarmed than impressed.

'Don't you like it?' I asked.

'Er, yes,' she said hesitantly, but the expression on her face said something different.

I realized that, for all her talk of how she wanted to piss her mother and stepfather off, her rebellion consisted of listening to music they hated, smoking the odd stolen cigarette and complaining about helping with the washing-up. That was as far as it was ever going to go.

'Come on, let's take our bikes and go into town,' I said, thinking we could mooch around the shops and have a Coke – I was dying to get a wider reaction to my new look.

She made up some excuse about having promised to help her mother, but I knew she simply didn't want to go.

'Sorry,' she said.

I turned on my heels and walked away.

That was the start of another lesson. Those who have something to lose guard it, while those who no longer value themselves are more careless about other people's opinions.

It did not take me long to find other more willing friends. If there were no other troubled children in the safe middle-class village where I lived, I knew there were in my uncle's, and I knew exactly where to find them.

31

The following week I was told I was going to spend another weekend at my uncle's house. Having another of those parties, I thought, as I listened to my mother talking on the phone, confirming the guest list and the dinner arrangements. That thought never failed to make me angry. But if she was pleased that I was staying away for the last weekend before school started, it didn't stop her tackling my uncle as soon as he walked through the door.

'What do you think you've been playing at?' she asked accusingly.

'What do you mean?' he said, glancing worriedly in my direction.

'Letting her buy those clothes and do this to herself.'

'Oh, come on, Dora,' he started to say, as he looked at her nervously.

I saw his hand go to his shirt pocket for cigarettes. Then, under my mother's steely glare, he remembered he was in a no-smoking zone and ran his fingers through his hair instead. 'She's growing up – anyone can see that,' he added.

'Well, don't give her money for any more! And don't let her touch her hair, except to wash some more of that colour out.' Every night she had stood over me, making sure I was shampooing it. As her hairdresser had predicted, the brightness of the red had faded during the week so that now I was more of a honey blonde with some patches of red still showing through, like the fur of a mottled ginger cat. I thought it still looked cool but I had been thinking of redoing it at the weekend.

'And no more makeup either,' she called after us as we left.

We drove to his house in silence. I didn't want to be there. I disliked the small dark rooms, the bare garden and my bedroom with its sparse, cheap furniture. Most of all I hated looking at the door that led to the room where my uncle kept his photographic equipment.

I knew he no longer wanted me to visit, but we were trapped. We couldn't explain to either his wife or my parents why that was. So he unwillingly became my accomplice as I exercised my right to my new freedom.

He dared not discipline me or bar me from going out. Over the weekends I stayed there, I was careful not to let my aunt know too much, just in case she thought it her duty to inform my mother that I was making a life over there. She had little knowledge of it but, whatever I was up to, she knew my mother would not approve.

Within a few weeks the smell of cigarettes clung to my clothes and my breath smelt of alcohol. Sometimes I thought my uncle must have felt as Dr Frankenstein had. He had created a monster for his own pleasure and was no longer in charge of it. I enjoyed watching him squirm at his impotence now that he had lost all power over me. I delighted in the fact that he was frightened of me, frightened of what I might do to bring down on him either the fury of my parents or, worse, the authorities.

He tried to warn me more than once: 'Jackie, your

parents might stop you coming here if they hear what you're up to.' Of course, he never actually said what he thought I was up to.

'As if I care,' I said, giving him my recently learnt stock reply.

'Well, you couldn't get away with so much at home, could you?' He was right.

But the need to smoke and then to buy those little white pills that made the world slip away became too strong. My body wanted more of whatever my uncle had fed me over the years, and I had found out how I could come by it.

After my transformation, when I visited my uncle's house it was only to change and go out again. There was a coffee shop, not the smart one where I had been on the day I went shopping, but a sleazy one. Fruit machines lined the walls and the place stank of rancid cooking fat.

On my first day back with my uncle that was where I headed. Wearing my new clothes and makeup, I sauntered in, trying to appear nonchalant as my eyes searched the crowd. I knew that what my mother called 'bad' teenagers hung out there and I wanted to meet some. I can't remember the sequence of events that followed, just that I soon made friends of a very different sort from either the 'nice' children at my school or the few who lived on our estate.

32

There was an area of flats and houses where the local council, in their wisdom, had rounded up 'problem' families. Single mothers whose children, by the time they started school, were bringing themselves up. Battered wives, who told the council they were escaping violent men but, in their new homes, took back their abusers. It was where a teenage boy's idea of a day out was sitting in juvenile court; a holiday was several weeks or months in a detention centre. The younger children were full of admiration for the ones old enough to do time.

Teenage pregnancy was rife; alcohol and drugs were freely available.

It didn't take me long to find my niche, or to discover how easy it was to pay for the drink and drugs. It started with a kiss and a fumble behind the garages, then it was a hand-job for a teenage boy – easy work to me. Sometimes we sat on piss-stained stairways, at others in flats where the parents had no interest in what their children did. There was an old church hall where, once upon a time, the newly arrived minister had tried to get the youth on the estate interested in various activities; the venture had failed dismally because his targets were apathetic and antagonistic to his cause.

So, whatever the weather, we found rooms, steps and corners where we could smoke and drink without interference. Girls who, with their makeup plastered on, looked older than their years went into off-licences and bought or stole what they wanted. I didn't care whether it was bought or stolen, I just enjoyed sharing it. Small pellets of marijuana were crumbled into tobacco, then turned into a bulky cigarette that, once lit, filled the air with a sweet, cloying smell. It would be passed round, and when it came to me I would drag the smoke deep into my lungs before handing it to the next person. Dope was more popular than alcohol but, then, it was even more forbidden than underage drinking.

And we all liked doing something that was forbidden.

The people in the group I had become friendly with all had a different story to tell.

There was Cathy who, at fourteen, played truant more than she attended school. Short, with chunky thighs, a row of studs adorning her ears and a tattoo of a snake around her arm, she was the one who was most vocal about her life. Her dad, she told me, was inside, not for the first time, it appeared. 'Got caught breaking and entering again, stupid bastard! Anyhow, I'm pleased to see the back of him,' she said. 'He used to beat my ma up. She'll take him back, though. She's a loser too. He'll get drunk, then come home and bash her about and I'll have to listen to him shouting and her screaming again. Then next thing they'll be all lovey-dovey and she'll be telling me that he loves her and it was just the fucking drink that did it. Yeah, sure – suppose the fucking drink blacked her eye. I don't think so! But do I care?'

She most probably did, but she was never going to admit it.

163

'Anyhow,' she told me, 'I'm leaving once he gets out. Getting my own place,' she added confidently, without saying how she was going to find the money to do so.

Then there was Mick, the fifteen-year-old son of an out-of-work coal miner. When I met him, I learnt that the woman my parents thought of as a national hero and miracle worker was considered a demon among my new friends. 'Put my dad and his mates out of work, closed the fucking pits, the Fascist cow,' said Mick, and a chorus of voices chimed in, blaming her for the strife and unemployment in the area.

I heard how some of the older ones had marched alongside the men, only to be forced back by police – another section of the community they were vitriolic about. 'Fascist pigs, they are,' Mick said fervently. 'My dad went to school with some of them, you know, but that didn't stop them charging at us. Oh, the papers said they moved them to different areas, but that wasn't true.'

I knew from my parents' discussions over breakfast that in fact it was, but I had no intention of saying so. On and on they went and the general opinion strongly aired was that the police had betrayed the working classes in which their roots also lay. Betrayed by the non-working ones as well, I thought, if what my father had said about some of the agitators in the picket lines was right, but again I kept quiet. Aping the opinions of their parents, the group spoke with the brand of wisdom that only those with limited knowledge possess.

Listening to them, my vocabulary extended even further. 'Bloody tossers,' I said in agreement.

I, who had heard that Margaret Thatcher was the

saviour of modern Britain, soaked up everything they said for it was all so contrary to the ideology of my parents and their Conservative friends. My new friends' talk was even better than the Johnny Rotten interview, I mused. Sensibly, I kept very quiet about my parents' views. But I also kept quiet about the detached house I lived in, the two-car garage that housed my father's large saloon and my mother's smaller one, and the fact that we had a cleaner – who, thankfully, did not live on the same estate as they did.

For the first time I encountered people who did not take money, or the things money can buy, for granted. My aunt and uncle might have said they both needed to work, but that was all. In that area most of my new friends' parents had to wait each week for the dole cheque to arrive. Either their mothers had to bring the children up on their own, living on state handouts, or their fathers had lost their jobs and become so despondent by the lack of employment in the area that they had given up looking for new ones. However, shortage of money was not something that appeared to bother my new friends. Unlike their parents, they had found ways of supplementing their incomes.

Shoplifting was one of the main sources. 'Going on the chore', they called it. 'Easy,' they told me confidently, when I asked how they did it. 'Just take the small things, bits of makeup and perfume, then drop them into your pocket. Small shops are the best. The bigger ones are getting wise and watch for it. You go in pairs, and while one of you is talking to the assistant, the other nicks the stuff.'

'Where do you sell it?' I asked curiously.

'At school, to posh kids like you who get pocket money,' they said, with a laugh.

They were curious about me: my accent betrayed my background. I told them my dad beat my mother. I still felt some loyalty to my parents and somehow I found it easier to tell stories that were not grounded in truth than to divulge the facts about the wife-swapping parties. Underneath I knew that, in their limited way, they had tried with me. But that did not stop the blind rage I felt at them. Neither did I want to admit that I knew my parents didn't love me for that would have labelled me as a loser. Although my new friends might have had to fend for themselves, and most of them thought their fathers were useless, they all showed some feelings for their mothers. Feelings I did not seem to possess. If she had loved me, she would have wanted me at home, wouldn't she? And if I had stayed there, my uncle would not have been able to do what he had done.

Round and round those thoughts went, only to be pushed to the back of my mind as I greedily held out my hand when the joint was passed to me and inhaled deeply. Dope, I found, made the world a happier place. Like the drugged drink my uncle had fed me for so long, it made the world blur – but differently. Even the weakest joke made me giggle uncontrollably. I could hear every note soaring out of tiny speakers and I was more aware of colours, which grew more vibrant.

If only I could smoke it when I was painting in class, I thought. I might get some really good stuff then.

It was on one of those weekends that I met Dave again, the boy I had met when I was five. The same boy I had been told was part of a dream and had known was not. He still had that unruly chestnut hair and was dressed in tight jeans. But this time his hair was styled and his jeans the new drainpipe ones. The softness of boyhood had left his body and his face. Over the years since I had met him he had shot up to nearly six foot tall. His shoulders were broad, and under his T-shirt, I could see the definition of muscle.

The cowed, defeated look he had worn when we had met was gone. Instead his face had hardened and there was a defiant bravado about him. It showed in the way he walked and even in how he stood. In his new self-contained confidence he appeared to be in his twenties, but I knew he could not yet have left his teens.

He might only have been a boy by legal standards, but in my new friends' eyes he was a man, one, I noticed straight away, who had captured their respect.

How we recognized each other after all that time, I do not know. But we did. Oh, not at first: it was my name that brought a look of recognition to his face. 'Is your uncle . . .?' and he said my uncle's name.

Shit, I thought. Then, as I studied him, I saw an older version of the boy I had met all those years ago.

'Yeah, but I'm having no more to do with him,' I replied, only to receive a disbelieving look.

'I mean not in that way,' I whispered. I looked away as my cheeks burnt with embarrassment. Of course I asked him not to tell. 'It was just that one time,' I lied.

'Oh, come off it, Jackie,' he said. 'I've heard about that uncle of yours. He and my dad –' He stopped, but I guessed he meant they had met again.

He said he had thought initially that I was his daughter, not his niece, and that seemed to make him angry. Then he did what he had done when I was five and he a few years older: he took my hand, laced his fingers through mine and squeezed gently. 'You all right?' he asked.

I told him that my uncle was too scared to touch me now. That something had happened – I didn't want to talk about it, but it had frightened my uncle. He was scared I might talk. 'Would you?' he asked.

I shuddered at the thought of reliving that time with the man and his whip. Just the fleeting memory of his face leering at me was enough to make bile rise into my throat. 'What? And have everyone know about me?' I answered. Our eyes met, and in his I read compassion and understanding. I knew I was not the only one who had something shameful to hide.

His breath was warm on my cheek as he said, 'Your secret's safe with me, Jackie. Don't worry, I'll not tell anyone.'

I leant against him, feeling that he was the one person who understood. His arm circled my shoulders and I allowed myself to feel comforted.

'I thrashed my old man, you know,' he said. 'As soon as I was big enough, I hit him. I'd worked out at the school gym so much that they thought I wanted to be an athlete. But all I wanted was to be big enough to stand up to him and to hit him if he came near me. And I did. He leaves me alone now, and my little sister. He had his eye on her too, the dirty bastard. You tell me if your uncle tries to start anything and he'll get sorted, OK?'

That was the start of a friendship that others thought should have been impossible, separated as Dave and I were by the gulf of years, but we were bound by our shattered pasts.

As I got to know the group better, I learnt that Dave was the main supplier of the drugs that were sold on the estate and in the schools. Some of the group worked for him, selling to their classmates as well as an assortment of people living on the estate.

I learnt that in the area, young as he was, he already had a reputation for being hard, and handy with his fists. One boy had found that out when he had helped himself to some of the white powder he was meant to be selling. Ed, his name was, a short, skinny boy with bad teeth and greasy hair. I found him unsettling. Eyes ringed with dark shadows would have told anyone well informed that his addiction was speed – whiz, as we called amphetamine sulphate, the poor man's cocaine. I was pleased that he was scared of Dave, for I had seen his eyes rake me up and down with a knowing sneer. It didn't take the others long to work out that, for some reason, Dave was my protector. Nobody was going to mess with me if he was around.

But whatever they whispered about Dave and his violence, I remembered the skinny boy with the dark bruises on his body who had skimmed stones across the river and tried to comfort me.

33

With him knowing me, although nobody guessed how, I was accepted. They knew I came from a different background and were curious as to why I wanted to hang out with them, but they just went along with it.

I stopped talking then and looked helplessly at my therapist. Even though nearly twenty years had passed since the day I had met the adult Dave, just talking about him still upset me. 'I know,' I said to her, 'that the only way to heal myself is to confront all of my past. To take all those memories that for so long I've pushed away and put them in order, then deal with them. But it's so hard to recollect everything I've tried so hard to forget.'

'You respected Dave, looked up to him, saw him as the one person who, knowing about your uncle, cared for you, didn't you?' she asked. Even though she knew the answer, her comment was framed as a question.

'Yes,' I said, 'I did. People who didn't understand said he was bad. But he was so damaged, so angry. And he took it out on the world.'

I wished then, as I spoke about him, that I could cry. For Dave deserved a tear, but I was unable to shed one for him.

My therapist waited for me to continue, then realized I needed some input from her. 'Jackie,' she said, 'unfortunately, frightened little boys who have suffered abuse often grow up into confused and angry men. And with some, that anger can turn to violence.' She sighed. 'The prisons are full of young men with sad pasts. Girls tend to turn anger towards themselves, with self-harming and bad relationships. It's tragic but true.'

'I just took it out on myself,' I said softly. I was thinking not only of the little scars left by cuts and cigarette burns but all the other things I had done to destroy my life. 'Once I watched an interview with an elderly woman who was a survivor of Auschwitz. She spoke about the horrors of what had happened there, of what she had seen, so dispassionately. She was so dignified, that wrinkled old woman. Not a tear ran down her face, nor was there a tremor of anger in her voice as she recounted how her whole family had been lost. She knew, I think, that when hate is mixed with loss it creates a poison that seeps through you until every part of you is contaminated by an anger so intense that your ability to function as a human being dissolves. If only Dave and I had understood that,' I said sadly.

A picture of Dave when he was still a boy slipped into my mind: he had been brave enough to protest at what the adults wanted us to do.

I remembered what he had been forced to do with me, and wondered what else he had been made to endure. I could only imagine. He had spoken of it to me only once and that was when we were older. But even then he had told me little.

I thought of his kindness to the women he had cared for: his mother, sister and me. But I also remembered how the other boys had feared him. I felt the wave of sadness

I always did when my mind visited the place where I kept his memory. Then I thought of the last time I had seen him, and his fate.

But I was not ready to talk about that. Not yet.

That, I thought, would have to wait for another session.

34

Was it just my desire for a leather jacket, or was it that the encroaching winter depressed me? Or was it another reason entirely that made my anger turn inwards so I wanted to hurt myself even more, to add degradation to the pain I inflicted upon myself? I used lighted candles to burn my skin and made tiny nicks with razors in places where they wouldn't show, but the pain no longer released me from the dark thoughts and dreams that haunted me at night.

I felt rage at my parents, a rage that expressed itself in sullen looks and a refusal to obey them. I was angry with my teachers and the other pupils for being happy, and even with Kat, who wanted less and less to do with me.

Maybe a combination of all that made me take the next step. It is not something I have ever been able to work out clearly.

Autumn had announced its arrival by turning the leaves of the oak trees a deep russet brown. Some had already fallen and they scrunched under my feet when I stomped angrily down the road. The trees always look their most beautiful, I thought, when their leaves are about to die.

In the morning there was frost on the cars, and as I walked to school my breath rose in wispy clouds.

The sun's rays had lost their warmth and daylight faded by late afternoon, leaving a misty grey twilight. Those gloomy days depressed me because they told me it was the run-up to Christmas. My aunt and uncle would visit us and I would have to act the role of a normal girl in a normal family.

For the last couple of weeks at school before we broke up, there would be a buzz of excitement. I heard plans being made, parties being arranged, which I knew I would not be invited to, as my classmates discussed what they considered to be the best time of the year.

At home I tried to catch sight of Kat but I was too proud to knock on her door. I didn't want to see her slightly impatient look as she muttered an excuse not to spend time with me.

There were occasions when she wanted to take her bike out and we would go together, but our friendship had faded. I had noticed she had also changed. Instead of the jeans she had once lived in, she had started wearing dresses. I had seen her laughing with her mother and stepfather as they had all climbed out of the car after what had clearly been a family day out. She loved the baby and often took him out in the pram for walks.

I had felt her stepfather looking at me with barely concealed distaste when he had seen me trying to catch her attention. I knew, without anything being specifically said, that it was partly his influence that had begun to end our friendship.

Maybe that was one of the reasons I wanted to be accepted by my new friends. Dressing like them was an important part of it. So was having enough cash to chip in my share for drink and marijuana. Since Dave had been seen to favour me, the boys who had once been happy to snog me in the shadows now kept a careful distance.

I really wanted a coat. Not the warm navy blue reefer jacket my mother had bought me – I would rather have died than be seen in that.

Definitely not cool, I thought. No. I wanted a leather jacket like Dave's, black, with a quilted lining and silver studs on the arms and collar. 'How much would one like yours cost?' I asked him.

He laughed at me. 'They don't do them in little girls' sizes,' he said dismissively.

But I wanted one, even if I had to get one a size too big.

'A hundred,' he admitted, when I refused to be fobbed off.

Where, I wondered, could I get that sort of money? But it was the overriding desire for the jacket that gave birth to my next step. I remembered the wads of notes I had seen men give my uncle. Cut out the middle man and get it for yourself, I thought. For if there was one thing my uncle had taught me, it was that there was no shortage of men who would pay to have sex with underage girls.

The first was a business colleague of my father's. I'd seen him looking at me when he had visited the house. I simply asked him for a lift.

'My, how you've grown,' he said, with the appreciative smile I recognized. 'How old are you now, Jackie?'

'Thirteen,' I lied.

'Boyfriend yet? Pretty girl like you must have one.'

I knew that jacket was coming nearer. 'Oh, I'm not really interested in boys,' I said, giving him a sideways look. Then I said the words that so many balding, paunchy middle-aged men dream of hearing from a pretty young girl. 'All the boys I know are just so immature.'

It took just a second for the stock answer I was to hear many times in the future to leave his mouth: 'Oh, if only I was twenty years younger!'

I wonder what difference you think that would make, I thought scornfully, but didn't show it. I lowered my eyelids and peeped at him through my lashes. 'Age doesn't matter, does it?' I said.

I earned twenty pounds for a quick grope and a promise that it was just between us.

My new career had started.

No more hand-jobs in exchange for a drink or a toke on a shared joint. I wanted more and I'd found it.

My reputation grew. I cannot remember who was next to slip two five-pound notes into my jeans pocket. I just remember he gave me ten pounds for doing much less than my uncle's friends had asked of me.

But I found – in my village and the one nearby, where nice, well-dressed young businessmen lived – there was indeed no shortage of men who would pay for sex with a girl of my age.

'How old are you?' they would ask.

I always added on a year to my age. 'Thirteen,' I told them. Thanks to the activities of a certain film director, thirteen, while not legal, drew the line between having sex with an underage girl and being a pervert who ogled children.

In their eyes I was a bit of naughtiness. To be fair, all of them were nice enough to me. No one asked for more than a hump in the missionary position. In first-time buyers' semi-detached and more affluent detached homes, when respectable young matrons and happy young mothers were out at PTA meetings, work or some charity event, I took off my clothes, lay down on their marital beds and spread my legs for their husbands.

They fantasized that I was into older men and that they were actually helping me avoid the clumsy embraces of inexperienced boys. They wanted to believe I was an innocent who should be allowed to learn the mysteries of sex from a skilled lover. Which, of course, they all imagined themselves to be, even the ones who had finished before I had counted the swirls on the ceiling, the roses on the wallpaper or whatever else I did to occupy my mind.

The money was just a small present, not a payment at all.

Well, they could believe what they liked. I wanted that jacket and, before the weather had turned much colder, I had it – plus a little store of notes for booze and dope.

'Birthday present,' I said to the shop assistant, as I chose the smallest jacket in the shop that would hang on my slight form.

Wicked, I thought, as I preened in front of the mirror. No other girl in the group has got one of these. I applied some makeup and, with a cigarette hanging out of my lipsticked mouth and a small wad of cash to buy what I considered essentials tucked firmly into my pocket, I sauntered into the coffee shop.

Being young, I had never given any thought to what those friends' lives were really like. I had no curiosity about how they lived during the hours I didn't see them or even once wondered about their dreams and ambitions. If I had given them more thought I might have seen that I had what they wanted, nice clothes and pocket money, for they didn't know how I came about my funds. However bad I had told them my home life was, they didn't see that my future would be the same as theirs: to live in the same dreary conditions as their parents.

I knew I had made a mistake when I saw the expressions on their faces. Instead of the admiration I had expected, there were sour looks.

'Where did you get that?' Cathy asked petulantly. 'Daddy bought it for you, did he?'

I knew some quick thinking was needed before I alienated them, but the truth was out of the question. 'Naw,' I said, with a mocking laugh I managed to conjure up. 'Don't be stupid. I nicked it. Said I was buying my boyfriend a wallet and when she was looking for one out the back, I stuffed this under my duffel coat.' They believed me, and I watched with relief as the disgruntled expressions turned to admiration.

But what did I really feel about the way I'd got that money?

It was certainly not what those men imagined when I was undressed and on a bed with them. I was angry – a white-hot anger – with my parents for never having noticed what was wrong with me, with my teachers for trying to understand but not seeing what was right in front of their noses, and with the experts, who told me I should be grateful for having so much.

That was what I felt – that and a growing hatred for all those men who lied to their wives, to me and to themselves.

But the hatred for them was nothing compared to the hatred I felt for myself.

35

The euphoria of being free, of being independent and what I thought was in control, did not last long. To begin with, I had waves of depression that continued until I was able to smoke a joint.

My nightmares grew worse, and in the morning when I looked in the mirror I felt that no one was there, just a blank white face staring out. There were days when my heart raced and my hands perspired and I woke filled with a nameless dread. Noise frightened me – the roar of traffic or the beeping of horns felt like an aggressive attack on my senses. When I had to pass people in the street I would duck my head and scurry by. Was it that I was scared of seeing one of my uncle's friends or, even worse, feel one of them, hidden in a doorway, watching my movements? I think it was. However much I tried to push their faces to the back of my mind, their images appeared as though they were burnt on to my retinas. My parents and the teachers thought that my blank looks when they spoke to me were just another show of defiance. But that wasn't it. It was just that I couldn't understand them. I would see mouths moving but I was unable to grasp the words they uttered and put them in order.

My problem with food came back, but this time it was even more severe. This time I wanted nothing inside me. I wanted to be empty, to make myself clean. The moment

I could get away from the table, I put my fingers down my throat, and when I retched, I kept them there until my throat burnt with the rush of vomit that splattered into the lavatory bowl. I forced myself to bring up everything that was in my stomach and kept my fingers there until only bile remained.

The only release I found came from the razors I hid in my room and the burns I inflicted on myself. When I couldn't find any candles, I would take my mother's curling tongs and plug them in; heated, I would hold them against the tender flesh under my upper arms.

The pain told me I existed, that the white face in the mirror was mine, and that I was alive. But it did not make me like myself.

The only time I thought I was happy was when I was able to drag down the smoke from a joint. Lying against a cushion in a friend's flat, standing in a shadowy corner, or on my own in a field as I blew it out through my nose, I would dreamily watch the curls of smoke drifting in the air as I felt my body relax.

But smoking dope created a paradoxical situation for a bulimic. Those indescribable munchies made me delve into the fridge at all hours. I would gobble down thick sandwiches stuffed with cheese and ham or whatever else I could find. Then, still not satisfied, my hands would reach for a dish of creamy dessert or I filled my mouth with bars of chocolate I had hidden in my room. Of course, later my fingers were again down my throat as I made myself throw up everything I had eaten.

'Don't you get enough at mealtimes?' my mother commented, when she saw the gaps in the fridge. 'Ah, well,

I suppose you're growing. You're just like your brother was at this age,' she would say grudgingly, as she looked with some bewilderment at my slight form.

At mealtimes, I tried to hide the fact that I could hardly bear the sight of food. I would push it round my plate, then, seeing my mother's eyes on me, force myself to place it in my mouth. That lump in my throat would stop it sliding down easily and I would feel it turning to mush. The knowledge that once the meal was over I could rid myself of it behind a locked bathroom door stopped me gagging.

There were even days when, having managed to take my bike out and roll a joint with recently purchased dope, I was able to eat everything that was put in front of me. On some occasions I even asked for more. 'Good to see you eating,' my mother would say.

I grew thinner over those months when I was relishing what I thought of as my freedom. At first it was put down to my age, and that I should be growing fast, even though I never did pass the five-foot-two mark. I liked being thin. I liked the way my clothes hung on me. I didn't want chunky thighs like Cathy's. More importantly, I didn't want food inside me. The thought of it horrified me. Large chunks of flesh, cream and cheese slowly turning to dirt. That was what made me place those fingers down my throat and vomit until there was nothing left. I suppose the drug I smoked kept me from wasting away. Some of the food from my binges must have managed to cling on so that, although I didn't grow fat, I didn't spiral down to skin and bones.

It's a pity I couldn't have explained that to the adult world when they found out about my drug habit. But when my parents did, they were certainly not in the mood to appreciate that particular benefit. That came later, after they decided I was ill. The words 'drugs' and 'bulimia' were not said. After all, twelve-year-old girls were not bulimic, were they? Maybe fussy eaters, but not bulimic. Neither did they take drugs – at least, not in our nice area. Nor were they suffering emotionally because of something the adult world had done to them.

They found out differently just before Christmas but the fact that I was ill was not admitted until the festivities were over.

36

The incident that had me admitted to hospital did not occur out of the blue. For several weeks, if not longer, I had been leading up to it. The black fog of depression had invaded my mind to the extent that even my parents were forced to notice. The darkness had lasted for several weeks before I finally admitted I needed help.

My parents first realized that something was really wrong and that things were coming to a head after I was brought home late one night.

My eyes felt glued together the following morning when I woke to a crashing headache and the salty taste of unbrushed teeth and stale alcohol. My sleep had been restless, my dreams chaotic, leaving the lingering fear that never seemed far away, and a blurred memory of the previous night's events. Gradually small pieces of the jigsaw floated into my mind. I remembered that I had mixed vodka, cheap cider and marijuana. I had wanted to make the world look different. Then what had happened? There was a blank where a memory should have been. How had I got back to my uncle's house? Had I stumbled back on foot or had someone given me a lift? A dim picture of Dave pulling me out of the flat I was in slipped into my mind. A group of us had been there, sitting around with dirty chipped glasses in our hands, bottles of drink all over the table and the floor, music blaring. Suddenly he had burst in.

I lifted my head off the pillow and, feeling too fragile to sit up, put my hands over my eyes. I tried to concentrate. The thin layer of dust that covered my memories lifted and, bit by bit, it all came back to me.

That week I had been more depressed than usual. If the start of winter with its run-up to Christmas was difficult to handle, then those days when it was just in front of me were worse. The day after school had broken up for the Christmas holidays, I had gone to where my uncle lived. None of the thoughts wandering through my head were happy ones when I had let myself into his house. On our own, he and I made no pretence of friendliness. On Christmas Day, though, when he and my aunt came to stay at my parents' house, I knew I had to slip back into the act that everyone thought was normal. The thought of having to give the expected kiss when I received my present, wish him a happy Christmas and pull crackers at the table, as though we were one big happy family, churned my stomach and made me feel nauseous.

That day, unable to stand my own company or his, I had wandered into town, trying to shake off my blues. It was full of people doing last-minute shopping. The shops had already started their sales. The supermarkets were open until late, carols blasted out through speakers arranged around a huge Christmas tree, and the moment dusk fell, the streets sparkled with hundreds of twinkling lights.

Young couples, engrossed in each other, their arms filled with packages, passed me, laughing. Women weighed down with brightly coloured shopping bags queued at the taxi rank. Sitting on a nearby bench, the older generation of the habitually unemployed, their brown teeth showing in what passed for a smile, drank cheap liquor out of bottles hidden in brown-paper bags. With the confidence of the inebriated, they called, 'Happy Christmas,' to everyone in earshot and looked vaguely indignant when no one returned their greetings.

All around me there was so much cheer and goodwill that it pulled me down even further.

I went into a shop that sold clothes, makeup and a variety of cassettes. Music and a new lipstick will set me right, I thought, as I walked in, only to find myself facing another huge artificial fir tree covered with silver bells and tinsel. By it sat a fat man with a false beard wearing a red suit that strained across his stomach. 'Fucking Santa,' I muttered, under my breath, as I watched rosy-cheeked children being given presents while their well-groomed mothers stood watching indulgently. 'Bet he's a sodding paedo,' I said to myself, as I glared sullenly at the happy scene.

But, then, that thought was never far from my mind. I used to wonder when I looked at men I saw on buses, sitting in coffee bars with their family or just walking along the street which of them abused children. I felt that every day I must have seen one but not recognized him. I knew better than anyone that a paedophile is not a seedy man in a dirty raincoat, with greasy hair and the shifty eyes that warn us to stay clear.

Paedophiles sit next to us on the bus, serve us in shops, teach children and work in banks. They look no different from the man next door and sometimes, of course, that is exactly who they are.

If I was honest with myself, I would have said envy was making me miserable. Everyone I saw looked happy, and I felt a seed of resentment germinating inside me. I wanted what they had: friends and parents who cared – and an uncle who was just that. I thought of going to the café and having coffee but I knew I would be sitting on my own, something I didn't want to do.

So, instead of staying in town and aimlessly whiling away a couple of hours, I went back to my uncle's house, helped myself to a full bottle of good vodka, which I placed in my duffel bag, and a half-bottle of something cheaper, which I put into my pocket. I took them round to one of the girls' flats. Jean, her name was, a mousy-haired girl who had recently left school, but so far had not managed to find work.

I needed a lift – 'Something to raise my spirits,' I told myself, and vodka would gain me entrance to Jean's house. In return, I knew Jean would share a joint or two with me. I knew that her mother, Rita, a skinny woman with bad teeth, skin the colour of cheap candles and the protruding stomach of a heavy drinker, would pounce on any bottle she saw. I made sure the one in my pocket was visible, but had no intention of mentioning the other, secreted at the bottom of my bag. I wasn't going to let her get her hands on that: it was for Jean and me to have later.

When I got to her flat, Rita was already drunk, with the lopsided belligerent stare that so often follows alcohol-induced good humour.

'Here! Give me some of that,' she said, pointing to the bottle she could see.

Jean took it from me and gave me a wink as she poured

her mother a stiff measure. 'That should do the trick, Mum,' she said, but I knew from her second wink that she meant it should finish her off and then we would have the sitting room to ourselves.

Good thing, I thought, when I saw the condition Rita was in, that I had had the presence of mind to hide the vodka. Otherwise we wouldn't have stood a chance of getting rid of her until either she had passed out or the bottle was empty.

Once the half-bottle was finished, mostly drunk by Rita, her bloodshot, blurry eyes turned to me. 'Got any cash with you, little rich girl?' she slurred.

Behind her Jean shook her head at me.

'No, only my bus fare,' I said, and received a snort of disgust.

Since there was no more drink in the house and no money to buy any, Rita took herself unsteadily up the stairs.

'She'll be there for the night,' Jean said, and, sure enough, within seconds we could hear Rita's rumbling snores. With her mother out of the way, we opened the second bottle and some Coke and put them on the scuffed coffee-table.

'What happens if she wakes up?' I asked, as Jean put a tape in the small stereo.

'She won't. She got her Giro this morning and she's been on the booze all day,' Jean answered.

As though some form of telepathy had told them that a bottle of vodka was in the flat, a group of teenagers, most of whom I knew, arrived, with bottles of cider. Joints were rolled and vodka poured. When a joint was finally passed to me, I held it to my lips and dragged as much of the smoke into my lungs as I could.

I could hear the bass vibrating, the thumping of the drums that almost drowned the words of the song on the tape that Jean had put on.

I lay back on the cushions as the electric guitar reached a deafening crescendo and closed my eyes. This is better, I thought.

'Here,' said one of the boys, breaking into my contented reverie. 'Open your eyes, Jackie – got something good for you.' I obeyed and looked over to where he was. A hand with nicotine-stained fingers was held out to me and I saw a couple of small white pills resting in the palm. 'You ever tripped, Jackie?'

I looked at him vacantly. I could tell by the challenging expression on his face that he was pretty confident of my ignorance. 'Yeah, sure,' I replied, having no intention of admitting that I didn't know what he meant.

'Liar,' he responded.

'I'm not!' I retorted.

He grinned, daring me, and gave me one of the pills – 'Swallow that, then.'

It looked harmless enough. I picked up a glass of vodka and Coke and quickly washed it down.

For a few minutes nothing happened. There was no buzz and none of that wonderful numb feeling. Just as I was beginning to think that the pill had been a joke at my expense, my eyes were suddenly riveted to my hands. I could see the bones under the skin, and when I moved my fingers they flashed different colours.

I giggled, then looked at Jean. Her eyes were huge and her hair streamed with the colours of the rainbow. I could feel everyone watching me, but I took no notice. Instead I looked around the room, just staring at different objects.

There was a picture on the wall, one of those prints in an imitation gilt frame of an exotic woman. Dark-skinned with thick black hair tumbling to her shoulders, she was wearing a gold dress that showed a generous amount of cleavage. I thought she was beautiful and, as I watched, her bright red lips smiled back at me.

As my gaze rested on the picture the woman's face changed. Lines appeared, scoring her forehead and feathering at the corners of her eyes. Her mouth caved in, and instead of white teeth I saw a dark cavity where they had fallen out. In front of me, her hair thinned, turned grey and brittle. In just a few seconds she was no longer young and beautiful but an old woman whom the ravages of time had marked cruelly. Eventually an ancient, toothless crone stared mournfully back at me.

The music swelled louder and louder until its reverberations filled my head and I placed my hands over my ears, trying to block out the deafening sounds. The room seemed to turn darker, the voices of those in it mocking. Still holding my hands over my ears, I glanced around frantically.

Someone had lit a candle, a red one that had been stuck into a chipped white holder. Beads of wax ran down – like drops of blood.

All of a sudden I wanted to leave the room and, with a rush of energy, I jumped to my feet. I was intent on getting to the front door, opening it and running into the night. Then I simply wanted to run and run.

Jean caught hold of me as I headed for the door.

'I need to get out,' I yelled, as I pushed at the arms that were trying to restrain me.

'You're just tripping, Jackie. You'll be all right in a bit,' she soothed me. 'What you fucking given her?' she shrieked at the boy, who was watching us with a smirk on his face.

'Just a tab, Jean,' he muttered, as he saw the fury on her face.

'What did you think you were doing? She's too young, you fucking idiot.' She gave me something to drink. 'Swallow that, Jackie, it'll help bring you down.' She held the glass to my mouth.

But when I looked at her, instead of the rainbow of bright colours that had glistened in her hair there were now streaks of blood, and the hand holding the glass was dripping with it.

I started to shake. 'Blood! It's blood!' I said.

'Put the candle out and gimme it,' she said, to one of the others. Then she showed it to me and explained it was just the wax melting that had made me think of blood. As her words sank in, they calmed me a little.

The room changed again. The music quietened, my panic subsided and the people faded into the background. Instead of seeing them, I found I was looking at a fairy scene. Without finding it odd, I saw Snow White with her dwarfs in front of me. 'Can you see them?' I asked.

'See what, Jackie?'

'Snow White! She's so pretty.' I reached out to touch her long diaphanous skirt.

'Jesus.' Jean forced more liquid down my throat.

That was when Dave arrived. He took one look at the

group and the state I was in, then threw everyone except Jean out of the flat. 'Scum bastards! Tossers,' he shouted at their retreating backs, before he attended to me. He put his hands on my shoulders and pressed down gently until I was sitting on the sofa. He sat next to me and held me gently. He talked me down from that trip, and when I had stopped hallucinating, he made me drink something – I think this time it was coffee.

It was Dave who took me to the bathroom, where I vomited all the alcohol I had consumed. After that he cleaned me up. Jean offered, but he refused, shouting at her for allowing this to happen. Then he shouted at me.

'For fuck's sake, Jackie! Do you want your uncle to have won?' Still feeling sick, I just looked at him, uncomprehending.

He caught hold of my shoulders again but this time he was not as gentle. He forced me to look into the mirror. I saw a pasty-faced girl, her hair falling in lank clumps around her face, her mascara forming black rings around her eyes. 'You look like a fucking panda. A stupid one,' he added, in case I thought I was forgiven. He gave me a light shake. 'Stop the drugs, Jackie.'

'You sell them!' I said, with the last ounce of defiance I possessed.

'Yeah – so what? Anyhow, it's weed I sell, makes you mellow – but you've been messing with other stuff. That's for losers. It'll do your head in.'

I tried to say that I could manage it, but I knew he was still angry so I nodded miserably.

He took me home with him, bundling me out of Jean's and dragging me round the corner to where he lived.

There, he said he had borrowed his father's car. 'He's asleep and you're not getting on the back of any motorbike in that state,' he said grimly, as he opened the passenger door. He placed his hand on the back of my head and pushed me in.

Yes, I remembered that, but not the drive. I must have dozed off. I had another dim memory of stumbling through the front door – and then I went cold as my mind told me something else. I took my hands away from my face and looked again at the familiar room I was in.

I wasn't at my uncle's house. I was at home.

Shit, I thought. Shit, shit, shit.

I had given Dave my parents' address.

I had woken them up, of course – they hadn't been expecting me. Now I remembered their shocked, angry faces and the shouting.

First they asked why I was there, then how had I got home, who had brought me, and wound up to 'What time do you call this?' and 'Just look at the state of you.' Then they realized that they wouldn't have approved of wherever I had been and there was more shouting.

'Where do you think you've been?' my mother had screeched.

'You'll come in at a decent hour!' my father had added.

'Leave me alone!' I had shot up the stairs to the sanctuary of my room.

The following day, little was said about my behaviour. Maybe they were too busy arranging Christmas – or maybe they were postponing their decision on what had to be done about me. But apart from telling me that I looked dreadful, they seemed to have made a pact not to talk about that night.

I cannot remember that Christmas, who my parents invited or what presents I was given, or how many times I made myself throw up. In fact I can't remember much of that time before I eventually woke up in hospital.

37

I have no recollection of the night when an ambulance, its blue lights flashing, turned into our driveway. It had been summoned urgently by our doctor, and I wondered how my mother had felt when the neighbours saw the unconscious form of her daughter being carried out of the house on a stretcher. I have no idea of what she told them when I didn't return home for a month. Nobody said and I never asked.

Maybe that white space where a memory should have been frightened me so much that I never sought to fill it. I have been told of that time, little bits of information imparted to me in stages, as I have of the following days and what happened thereafter. It has mixed with my own memories until I am unable to separate which are mine and which were given to me by someone else. All I know is that it happened.

I learnt, much later, that it did not take long after that night for my parents to seize on the excuse, with apparent relief, that what was wrong with me was not their fault. The psychiatrists all agreed I had a mental illness, although they disputed among themselves as to what name it should be given. They agreed on one other thing when they talked to my parents: it had been caused by something outside their control.

The consensus was that my troubled mind was nothing

to do with the adult world. My parents had never made me feel unwanted and unloved, had they? But I might have been born with a problem, a weakness, that had manifested itself as I developed.

How about a split personality, or dissociative identity disorder, as it has since been named? That seemed, in light of my actions that night, to be possible. Or perhaps it was even schizophrenia, which often showed itself with the onset of the teenage years. Nowadays, with all the medical breakthroughs, that could be treated – or, rather, controlled with drugs. The NHS could become my new supplier.

So, there really wasn't a lot to worry about; unfortunate, of course, but not insurmountable, and certainly not my parents' fault. That was the eventual diagnosis, which must have given them so much relief. Without having had to confess any acts of bad parenting, they had been absolved of blame.

I was thirteen.

38

I was frightened – frightened of the deep depression that enveloped me, as though a damp dark fog had wrapped itself round my limbs and curled round my mind, stifling it. It obscured my vision of day-to-day living, visited me at night and woke me each morning with its mocking scorn at my futile efforts to live my life.

As soon as Christmas was over, I knew I could no longer cope. I had thought of suicide, of taking one of the blades from my father's razor and slashing at my wrists until I opened one of the blue veins I could see beneath my skin. I imagined that I would then sit and watch, almost curiously, as my blood ran out slowly, taking my life with it. Or should I look for a supply of those pills, the white ones that made me relaxed and sleepy, and swallow them all one night?

I imagined a dreamless sleep and then nothing. That was what filled my thoughts constantly over those weeks.

But in the times when the fog lifted and glimpses of something intangible, maybe a shaft of light, indicated that I might have a future, I resisted its demands. There was inside me a tiny kernel of hope that once I reached the magic age of sixteen I could walk into adulthood and escape everything oppressive in my world: my uncle's presence and my parents' disapproval.

So when that small spark of optimism came, I knew

I wanted to see adulthood and explore what those years might bring. I might learn to drive a car, listen to music in a disco, have a circle of friends, and one day even find someone to love – someone who in turn would love me. I decided that I was going to fight the fog and not let it take away a future that just might be good.

Coupled with those flashes of optimism, there was a fear: fear of what I might do before I found it was too late to turn the clock back. It was this that made me admit to my mother I was ill.

I was not prepared to tell her the full extent of the illness that caused those dark thoughts and the hopeless despair that stalked me. I informed her that I thought there was something wrong with me, that I was vomiting again as I had done as a child. I omitted to tell her that my own fingers were the cause of it. But I wanted a reason to visit the doctor and I wanted to go alone.

'Can you make me an appointment?' I asked. 'I can take myself there,' I added, trying to give the impression that I was being considerate. My mother gave me a searching look, then said she would make the phone call.

I wanted to talk to someone whose opinion of me was not coloured by what my parents had told them. To the best of my knowledge, the doctor had only seen me for childhood ailments. Of course, then I didn't know about medical records and that every appointment made with the psychologists had been recorded and sent to the GP I was so desperate to see.

Neither did I know that my parents had already been talking to him about me. I had no idea that they had already made enquiries about me going into residential care; my father was still opposing it, but with less vigour each time I showed another sign of being out of control.

An appointment was made for the following day.

As soon as the surgery opened, I was there. I sat in the waiting room flicking through ancient magazines, anxious to get it over with. 'He has a patient with him,' the receptionist told me, when I asked how long he was going to be. 'He'll see you next.'

My mother, not a patient, had been with him. Through the window of the waiting room I saw her, head down, leaving by the back door. She must have thought I wouldn't notice her as she scuttled out, but I did.

I was full of rage. I believed she would have poisoned him against me, that it would now be pointless to ask him for help. But I decided to try anyway.

'I'm depressed,' I told him, once I was seated in his room. 'I have bad dreams,' I added. 'Things frighten me,' I said, averting my eyes. There, I thought. That was more than I had ever admitted before – so where was the prescription pad for him to write on? There must be something he could give me that would make me feel better.

Instead of the concern I had been hoping for, he looked at me impassively, then talked about teenage hormones. He asked if my periods were regular and, of course, when the last one had been.

Just checking, I thought, to make sure I'm not pregnant. He took my pulse, said everything appeared to be in order and told me how lucky I was, good parents, nice home, et cetera. When he had finished talking about my burgeoning hormones, he scribbled on the pad, which had been hiding in a drawer, and handed me a prescription for a tonic.

'That should sort you out,' he said gruffly, and then I was out of his surgery with nothing accomplished.

Could no one hear me? Could no one see I needed help? But, of course, no one could.

That night was the first time my angry, terrified five-year-old self appeared. She stepped out of my body, ready to scream and shout at the world that had betrayed her.

My parents had witnessed, when I was younger, the toddler me, the one who had talked in a baby language and rocked herself against a wall, but then the word 'regression' had been bandied about. This time there was no mistaking it. They realized that something was seriously wrong.

I had completely disappeared when my younger self put in her appearance. Gone to a place where my thoughts, my hearing and all sense of who I was vanished. And the little girl who sat in her room likewise had no recollection of me. At first she was quiet, a good child who brought her teddy bears down from the shelves, where for several years they had lain neglected, and placed them in a corner. She sat down with them, picked up the one that had been her favourite, Paddington, and cuddled him.

It was when my mother called me to come down for my meal that I was found. Annoyed at what she thought was bad behaviour, she had climbed the stairs, marched to my room and, without knocking, unceremoniously flung open the door. There she was faced with a small child in her thirteen-year-old daughter's body. At first the child refused to speak, just sat holding Paddington, and looked at the woman with something akin to bewilderment. Realizing that the mother's initial anger was turning to worry, she tried to utter a few words. Her speech was different. Her voice was higher and her vocabulary smaller. For a few moments, my mother thought I was playing some sort of malicious game.

I can imagine her impatience, how she tried to snatch Paddington from my arms, how she shouted, forgetting that five-year-olds are more easily frightened than older children. But she had not accepted that that was who she was dealing with.

That realization came when the child in front of her opened her mouth and bawled, face red with approaching temper. My mother took a step back, still unsure of what was happening. Then the child ran across the room screaming and, as she had done at five, threw herself against the wall, filling the room with ear-piercing, anguished cries.

I was not witness to that or to my mother wrestling me to the floor and yelling for my father. Neither was I there when the doctor arrived and slid a needle into my arm.

I have no memory of the ambulance arriving or of the journey to the hospital.

I only know that when I woke there was no sign of my five-year-old self. I didn't know she had ever been there. All I knew when I opened my eyes was that a woman's face I did not recognize was hovering just above my head.

39

She told me I was in hospital, that I had been brought in the night before. She explained that I had not woken up when they had put me to bed, and that I had slept through the night. On and on she went in her calm, reassuring voice, which, within just a few seconds, had begun to grate on my nerves.

'What's wrong with me?' I asked, and before she could answer, I blurted out another question: 'How did I get here?' As those words left my mouth, I felt a rising sense of panic. I had no recollection of the events of the previous night – and that scared me. It was much worse than the time Dave had brought me home, for then I had had some blurred images. This time there were none.

'You came by ambulance last night,' she said matter-of-factly. But that did not tell me why, and I clutched the bedclothes with hands that suddenly felt damp as my fear rose and I tried to remember. 'Doctor will explain everything,' she told me, when she saw the anxious look on my face. I tried to ask more questions, but she just patted my hand, said that the doctor would be along soon and that he would explain everything.

A cup of warm, milky tea was brought to me and I was asked if I was hungry.

'No,' I said. My stomach felt as though it had been invaded by a swarm of butterflies beating their wings.

No comment was forthcoming. Instead, after helping me to the toilet, the nurse told me to stay where I was and get some rest. The curtains were drawn round my bed as she left. On the way to and from the toilet I had caught sight of nurses in uniform and people in dressing-gowns, who must have been patients, but in my confused state they had hardly registered. Through the curtains I could see vague shapes of people and hear voices, but something stopped me pulling the curtain aside to see what was behind it.

As the nurse had indicated, a doctor arrived soon afterwards. Not a man with a stethoscope around his neck and a white coat: instead he was dressed in casual clothes, light trousers, an open-neck shirt and a jumper. He was younger than the psychologists I had seen before, fresh-faced with floppy brown hair that he flicked back. Brown eyes met mine as he gave a warm smile that was meant to reassure me.

It didn't.

He sat on the chair next to my bed and told me I could call him Peter. 'We don't stand on formality here,' he said, and added that he was a psychiatrist. I had already worked that out the moment he had introduced himself. Well, it stood to reason – his casual clothes and the use of his Christian name had given me a pretty strong clue that this was no ordinary 'doctor'.

'I know from your parents that I'm not the first one you've met,' he said, 'so there's nothing to be scared of, is there?'

I wasn't too sure of that. His job was to look into people's heads and I didn't want mine examined too closely.

I pulled up my bedclothes and looked at him with what I thought was a helpless expression. Whatever had happened the night before, I wanted to get out of this place. The fact that he was a psychiatrist told me what sort of ward I was in and I didn't want to spend any time with crazy people. I mentally crossed my fingers and hoped he would be a pushover.

He wasn't.

I asked the questions I had asked the nurse and expected to hear some soothing words that would put my mind at rest. Instead he glanced down at his notes, looked up and gave me another smile, one I didn't trust.

'I realise, Jackie,' he said, 'that you have a lot of questions for me, but let me ask you a few first. All right?'

No, it wasn't all right, but he didn't give me a chance to object.

'Let's talk about drugs, Jackie,' was the first thing he said to me and, caught completely unawares, my mouth dropped open in shock.

I had a sinking feeling then that the conversation he had in mind was not one that I wanted to pursue.

I tried to play for time and turned what I hoped was an innocent face towards him. 'What do you mean?'

It didn't work.

'Drugs, Jackie,' he repeated. 'The ones you've been taking.'

No point in denying it, I realized, when he told me marijuana had been found in my room.

Oh, wonderful, I thought. My mother must have had a field day going through everything. I had hidden it and the little packet of cigarette papers underneath one of the teddy bears. Of course, I didn't know then that my five-year-old self had betrayed me by lifting them all down and leaving my dope and papers clearly on display.

'And your mother found some pills,' he added.

Bloody hell! I thought. She found those Mandies. Oh, shit!

I tried to bluff my way out of that. 'They're just pain-killers,' I said, 'for period pains.' Men, I knew, didn't like to talk about girls' menstrual cycles and I thought that would shut him up.

Wrong again.

'Don't take me for a fool, Jackie. "Mx" stamped on them means Mandrax. I suppose you've been mixing them with the dope.'

I looked at his face, which showed neither criticism nor approval. What I saw was an implacable determination to get to the bottom of the facts of my life.

It wasn't going to be as easy as I'd imagined to pull the wool over his eyes. I knew when I saw the firmness behind his smile that I hadn't managed, even for a second, to hoodwink him with my expression of innocence mixed with confusion.

'Well, I did take them for pain,' I protested, but I knew I was not believed.

More questions followed. They were so fast that I had little time to think how to answer them. Where had I got them from, who had given them to me and how often did I use them?

'Just some kids I met,' I said. Answering the second question first and ignoring the other two. No, I didn't know their names, I told him, and, no, they were not at the same school as me. I had met them at a coffee shop.

'How did you pay for them?'

Again I tried the innocent look. 'They gave them to me,' I said, for I certainly didn't want to answer any questions about how I had found the money.

'Come on, Jackie,' he said. 'I know a joint might be passed round but the Mandrax your mother found isn't cheap, so you've got to be buying stuff, haven't you?'

I told him that this was the first time I had paid for anything and that I had used my pocket money and taken some money from my savings. 'I do get money as birthday and Christmas presents,' I said, with what I hoped was the right amount of righteous indignation.

Whether he believed me or not, he decided to move on. 'Now,' he said, 'what do you remember about last night?'

I told him I had no idea what had happened that had caused me to be taken to hospital.

He told me a little then. 'Your mother found you in your room playing with your teddy bears. You were acting as though you were only about five,' he said, and this time his voice was guarded. I knew there was more that he was not telling me.

'Has anything like that ever occurred before? Maybe after you took some pills. You know, sometimes they can make you see things that aren't there, especially if you mix alcohol and dope with them.'

I thought of the tab I had taken, but decided not to share that particular piece of information with him. 'No,' I said emphatically.

'Well, did you take anything last night?'

'No,' I said. But if he thought it was the drugs that had made me act the way I had, and if I promised not to take them again, maybe they would let me go home. 'Well, per-haps I might have, I don't know. I can't remember. But I must have, I suppose,' I said quickly. I babbled on a bit more about how I didn't know they were harmful, they must have been what had caused my behaviour and I wouldn't do it again. Then, pleased with my effort, I gave him a conciliatory look. Now he'll have to let me go, because there's nothing wrong with me, I thought.

Wrong! As far as he was concerned, I hadn't got one thing right. My history went too far back and he was not in the least bit convinced that I was telling the truth.

Other questions were fired at me, and I realized that again he had seen through my subterfuge.

Bloody hell, I thought. Aren't psychiatrists supposed to be kind rather than interrogators? Resentful at his lack of trust, I tried to slip deeper under the bedclothes.

'Sit up, Jackie,' he said, 'you've slept enough. Now, you went to see your family doctor yesterday, didn't you?'

I said nothing, for he clearly knew I had.

'You told him you were depressed. Why was that?'

I clammed up. If he knew that, he already knew what I had told the doctor and I wasn't going to add to it. I shrugged as much as the bedclothes would let me. 'I suppose I was,' I said eventually, then asked him the one question I wanted an answer to. 'I feel fine now! When can I go home?'

He ignored that and returned to the subject of drugs. He said how harmful they were and that the people who had given them to me were not friends. It was a fact that people who used drugs themselves liked to get other people to join them. After the lecture he focused on my parents and how worried they were about me. I switched off. I knew that speech too well and it would end as it always did, with words expressing how lucky I was.

I saw him watching me. He steepled his fingers and rested his chin on them as he studied my face thoughtfully. He's trying to work out if I'm sick or just plain bad, I thought, and stared back at him with a blank expression.

I wasn't going to let him see that I was scared.

'All right, Jackie, you can relax. That's enough for now,' he said finally, after a long period of silence.

'When can I go home?' I asked again.

'We'll talk about that the next time I see you.'

I had meant what time, not which day.

'I'm not going home today, am I?' I said. I tried to keep my voice calm – a simple fact needed confirmation – but it didn't come out that way. Horrified, I heard the shaky tremor and the high note of worry and knew they showed I was afraid.

He glanced at me and I saw a degree of sympathy in his eyes. That worried me more than disdain would have done. If he felt sorry for me, it meant he believed there was something wrong with my head. Didn't it? At that thought the swarm of butterflies started fluttering around in my stomach again.

'Your father's bringing in some clothes for you, so you can get dressed as soon as they arrive. The nurse will show you around.' And before I could protest that he hadn't answered my question, he left.

As though on cue, no sooner had he made his exit than my father appeared. I suspected he must have been waiting for the doctor to leave.

'How are you feeling this morning, Jackie?' he asked, in the forced, bright tone that the nurse had used.

'All right, I suppose,' was the only answer I could think of, as he sat on the chair the doctor had just vacated. He seemed to be more awkward than angry, which I guessed, as she hadn't come, my mother was. He looked tired and, if I could have thought of the word then, defeated.

'Your mother's packed you your dressing-gown and some clothes,' he said, without mentioning why he, not she, had brought them. The worried look I so hated was back on his face. His fingers involuntarily rubbed the deepening crease at the top of his nose, between his eyes, and I saw that he looked suddenly older. I felt a pang of guilt, for I knew my behaviour had caused that.

'Jackie,' he said, 'do you remember anything about yesterday evening at all?'

I shook my head. I remembered going to the doctor and coming home angry, but that was all. 'No, what happened?' I asked.

'What did the doctor tell you?'

I sensed that he didn't want to give me more information than I already had. 'Not much, but he wasn't there, was he? He just said that I seemed to think I was five.' I looked at him nervously, wondering what else had happened that had made them send for an ambulance.

'Well, you did seem a little confused,' he said. 'You gave us a bit of a fright. But you seem much better now.'

He told me nothing else. Instead he talked about how I wasn't well and how the hospital would get me better again. His words were meant to placate me, but as he said them, I wondered if the expression 'not well' was a euphemism for something much more serious. I searched my father's face for some sign of the true meaning, but it gave nothing away.

'Have you found everything you need?' he asked, once I had rummaged through the bag to see what he had brought. Underneath my clothes were my Walkman and a selection of cassettes. This touched me, for I knew that he, not my mother, had packed them.

'My music! Thank you, Daddy,' I said. Maybe it was because I had shown some gratitude that he suddenly remembered the girl I had been before I had turned into the problem child.

'Jackie,' he started to say hesitantly, as he placed his hand gently on mine. He seemed about to ask or say something significant, but whatever it was, he reconsidered. 'Is there anything else you want brought in?' was all he said.

No, I thought. I don't want anything brought in. I want you to take me out of here. I wanted to say, 'Please take me home. I'll be good if you do,' but the words stuck in my throat. Instead, I mumbled that I didn't need anything. Now I had a sinking feeling. Bringing things in didn't sound as though my father had any intention of saying that I could go home with him in the foreseeable future.

'How long am I going to be here?' I asked, trying to sound nonchalant.

'Just until you're feeling better. You're in good hands, Jackie,' he said. He looked at his watch, keen to escape being pushed further. He patted my hand and muttered something about a business meeting, then took out his wallet, peeled off a couple of five-pound notes. 'In case you think of anything after I've gone,' he said, 'there's a shop in the foyer. The nurse will take you there.' Then, with an awkward look that barely disguised his relief, he got up and left.

Now it was the nurse's turn to come into my space. 'I see you've got your clothes, so you can get up now, Jackie. Let's get you bathed first, though,' she said, in the irritating bright voice I already loathed.

I pulled on my dressing-gown; wearing something of my own made me feel marginally better. She led the way to one of the bathrooms where I spent as long as I could, delaying coming out. I soaped every inch of myself, lathered shampoo on my head, then ducked under the water to rinse it off. I splashed a lot to let her know I hadn't drowned myself. But I couldn't delay coming out for ever. A knock and the nurse's voice confirmed that.

'Time to get out now, Jackie,' she called.

Cursing her under my breath, I climbed out and rubbed myself dry.

'Now, dear,' she said, handing me a hair-drier, 'as soon as you've done that and put on some clothes, I'll show you around.'

'How long am I staying?' I asked, thinking that she might know and tell me.

'It's up to the doctor,' she replied, echoing my father's words.

Suddenly the frustration of not knowing what was happening was too much. 'What's wrong with everyone that they can't fucking well answer me?' I yelled.

My outburst had no effect. 'Come on, Jackie,' was all she said. 'Get yourself dressed.'

I glared at her, then grudgingly decided that my day clothes would be better than a hospital nightdress and my dressing-gown.

As soon as I had wriggled into my jeans and pulled a T-shirt over my head, I discovered that my Dr Martens were missing. Instead, a pair of soft-soled slippers was the only footwear in my case. 'I haven't got my shoes,' I told her.

'Well, you don't need them in here, do you?'

Still wanting to put off whatever she had in mind for me, I told her that I wanted to go to the shop. 'My father gave me some money to buy a few things,' I said.

She raised no objection, took me to the lift and we went down to the ground floor. She walked so close to me that I knew she was not going to leave my side. That told me I had no chance of leaving the ward alone.

The shop, although small, seemed to stock everything: bunches of flowers for visitors who needed to make a last-minute purchase, paperbacks, toiletries, magazines, plus an assortment of sweets and fruit. Under her watchful gaze, I bought a magazine and, unable to think of any more excuses to waste time, I followed her reluctantly back to the ward. She then took me on the promised guided tour. First to the dining room, furnished with long tables and plastic chairs; she told me the mealtimes.

Anyone would think I was in a fucking hotel, I thought, but some grain of common sense told me to keep my thoughts to myself.

'You know where the bathrooms are now. You can have a bath each morning,' she told me, then added that they were kept locked, but a nurse would let me in.

The next stop was the 'lounge': a large, square room with pale yellow walls, a television in the corner and a few tables. An odd collection of lumpy armchairs was dotted around the room and an assortment of people, wearing tracksuits, were sitting in them.

She introduced me to a few people, who showed little interest in me, then said she would leave me there to relax.

Glancing around I saw that few people were doing more than staring into space. In fact, they looked as though they were on something a lot strong than the Mandies I took when I really wanted to chill out. Maybe it's not going to be too bad in here after all, I thought, but I didn't believe it.

As the morning passed, the other inmates showed animation only when the trolley arrived with a choice of weak tea or coffee and some cheap biscuits. The latter they piled on to plates and took back to their chairs.

Eavesdropping on some of their sporadic conversations, I heard a few reasons why some were in there. Divorcees had depression, and people with high-powered jobs had cracked under the pressure. Those seemed the most common.

A man who looked less zonked out than the others told me how he had got out of his car in a rush-hour traffic jam and left it at the end of a flyover with the doors locked and the engine still running. 'I'd had enough. I just got out and walked away. Must have caused chaos,' he said proudly, as though bringing the city to a standstill was something to be commended.

I was intrigued, though, and asked what had happened.

'The police got it blown up. Thought it belonged to an IRA bomber.' He laughed.

There were only two people in the room who, although older than me, were at least in the same decade. One was a student who looked suspiciously thin. Bet he's been sniffing the white stuff, I thought. I knew how much of it Dave sold to students at a well-known university. There, third-year students, having partied too hard for two years, had to work all night to get ready for the exams. Whatever he had taken, he looked burnt out and clearly had no interest in talking to a thirteen-year-old.

My eyes kept resting on a boy. He was slumped in a chair, his head nearly resting on his chest, as though his neck wasn't strong enough to support it. Dark hair hung over a pale face, and beneath his jumper sleeves, I could see his thin, bony wrists. They were newly bandaged, and I knew what he had done. His fingers, the only part of his body that looked alive, curled and uncurled. Later, when I passed him, I heard him humming a toneless melody to which only he knew the words.

'What's up with him?' I asked the man who had walked away from his car. Although I had taken a dislike to him, he was the only person who did not appear completely adrift in a world outside the walls surrounding us.

'Lost his parents in a car crash, poor little bugger. He won't talk. They'll shock him if he carries on like that,' he said, with some relish, as he lit a cigarette and blew a cloud of smoke into my face.

Seeing my puzzled look, he explained, 'They'll run electricity through his head. That'll get him talking, all right.'

I said nothing. I thought he just wanted to scare me.

That first day I watched the other people with a sinking dread. Apart from the ones who were so depressed that tears ran down their cheeks as they chain-smoked, there were people who laughed out loud for no reason. Others talked to themselves, standing in corners and muttering away as though whoever lived in their head was a lot more interesting than the people around them.

Mind you, when I looked at what was available in the way of a conversation, I couldn't really blame them.

The patients seemed curiously sexless. The men's walk had little of the usual masculine swagger, and the women didn't move daintily or wiggle their hips. Instead they shuffled as though their legs had grown heavy and cumbersome. There were no flirtatious glances, no eyes meeting with awakening desire that normally happens when enough people of both sexes are together in a confined space.

No: depression or medication had made eunuchs of us all.

There was one exception to the 'I'm depressed so I don't care what I look like' brigade. She was a woman on the tail end of what my mother called middle age, who caught my eye as she entered the room. The only person apart from me not wearing a shapeless tracksuit, she was in black trousers and jumper. There were pearls around her neck and in her ears, her blonde hair was swept up, her blue eyes were carefully lined with black, her dark lashes were spiky with mascara, and the nails at the end of her wrinkled fingers were scarlet.

Seeing me – or, rather, as I learnt, a new audience – she

sat near my chair, prepared to be entertaining. Nearly every sentence that left her mouth started 'When I was a model', or 'When I was being photographed on a shoot', or 'When I was walking down the catwalk'. Well, I got the idea!

'I was well known!' she said to me, in a surprised voice, when she noticed the blank look on my face.

If she had told me she was an old rocker, say, and had once dressed, like Suzi Quatro, from head to toe in leather, and done drugs, I might have been interested, but a model walking up and down in silly clothes?

'Oh, well, you're too young, I suppose,' she said dismissively, and turned her head away.

'She's telling the truth,' the man who had abandoned his car said. 'She used to be a real beauty.'

I must have looked sceptical: at thirteen, anyone over thirty looked old to me and Old Father Time had not been particularly kind to her.

'Well, apart from three marriages and a lot of affairs, there's been a lot of gin and cigarettes along the road she's travelled – but she was a stunner in her time, all right. She used to make the headlines when she went into some fancy private clinic to dry out. Shame the money dried up before she dried out,' he said, cackling at what, in his book, passed for wit.

'So, the same for her as us. It's the National Health now,' he said complacently.

Wanting to drown his voice, I put on my headphones and turned up the sound. He gave up on me and ambled aimlessly away.

Oh, for a joint, I thought, and wondered if I could get to a phone and ring up Dave. He'd bring me something.

'No phone calls and no visitors except your parents,' I was told, when I made my request.

My days there were so boring. With visitors banned and just my parents turning up – being seen to do their duty, I thought – the time stretched endlessly in front of me. My mother, sitting awkwardly in one of the uncomfortable chairs, trying to think of something to say to me, was not a visitor I looked forward to seeing. By the end of an hour – less would have looked uncaring and longer would have used up all her conversational resources – she gathered up her handbag, planted a dry kiss on my cheek and made a dignified exit.

I can't remember what we talked about, only the relief when she left.

Her visits took up six hours a week, and once a week both of my parents arrived, carrying parcels of whatever I had asked for, mainly music. They tried bringing books and I did make some effort to read them, but my ability to concentrate, which had never been great, seemed to have deserted me. That visit also lasted an hour.

Bathing and fiddling with my hair took up at least sixty minutes every day, eating accounted for another ninety, and then there was an hour with Peter. When I added it all together my day was fuller than I had expected.

The rest of the time I spent listening to some of the other patients. Nobody had much that was interesting to talk about.

Anyhow, being screwed by my uncle and his friends, photographed, whipped and peed on topped any of their pathetic stories, I thought resentfully. There were not many kind thoughts in my head then.

My anger at being in hospital showed in my sullenness towards the nurses, my lack of co-operation with the doctors, and my refusal to eat more than a tiny amount at meals.

What they couldn't see, though, was how scared I was. For the question I kept asking myself was, What will happen if I don't get better? The poor boy who had lost his parents and attempted suicide didn't appear to be making much progress. He was still not speaking or even showing any recognition of the people who tried to talk to him. He never did say anything, not once during the four weeks I spent there. Day after day, I would see him gazing at the walls until a nurse came and touched his arm. Without making eye contact, he would get up and follow her.

I wondered what would happen to him. I watched visitors come to see him, place caring hands on his, whisper soft, comforting words, but he stayed locked in the place that exists within the mind, which no one can penetrate to cause any more hurt.

And, of course, I was worried about what was wrong with me. I was scared that I would be tricked into telling them the things I didn't want them to know, which made me monosyllabic, or almost, when answering questions. 'Who can eat this muck?' was my standard reply when asked why I had left so much food on my plate.

My behaviour during those early days in the hospital was not scoring me any Brownie points. When I was asked to take part in quiz games or anything else, I would walk away, jam on my headphones and listen to Metallica, especially 'Sanitarium'. I played it over and over.

I can still remember the words: they were about being

mentally ill and seeking freedom. The song summed up my state of mind. The trouble was, my freedom wasn't in sight, and underneath my bravado, I was scared.

What if I was so ill, I had to stay there for the rest of my life?

40

The curtains around my bed swished back and a girl a few years older than me, with hair the colour of corn and deep blue eyes, stood there. 'Jackie,' she said, 'I know. I don't know who it was, probably your father, brother or a neighbour. But I know.'

I opened my mouth to speak and she placed a finger gently on my lips. 'Shush,' she said. 'Listen to me and take my advice. You're angry, very angry, and so full of hate. Let it go. You think you're bad, but you're just a hurt child.'

Her hand rested against my cheek, a caress, and I turned my face towards it.

'I understand,' she said. 'I understand what you're going through.'

I knew she spoke the truth.

'Who are you?' I managed to ask.

'Tonight,' she replied, 'just think of me as your angel.' Then, leaning close, she whispered what I must do if I was going to leave the ward. 'You see, Jackie, it was anger that brought you in here, and it's anger that's keeping you here. The more you protest, the more they will scribble in their files that you're too ill to leave. Be good, pay attention and listen to your therapist.'

'What will you do to leave here?' I asked.

'Who says I want to?' she replied.

'They think there's more than one person inside my

body,' I said at last, putting into words what I knew to be true.

'So what?' she replied. 'It's better than only having one – that's for ordinary people, and you don't want to be ordinary, do you?'

I shook my head slightly.

'Jackie, we're all a little split, so what are you worried about? A frightened little girl comes out and is angry because no one helps her? She'll go away one day, when you make her safe. But, Jackie, that rebellion of yours must be like the wind that finally blows itself out. Up to now, it has been like a gale, or a great storm. Now you must let it drift away and be calm. Do you understand?'

I did.

She climbed on to the bed and lay beside me. Her soft arms wrapped themselves around me, and for the first time in that place, I felt comforted. My head rested against her breast, my nostrils filled with her light perfume, and as I drifted off to sleep, I felt her lips gently press against my head. When I woke, she was gone.

'Who is she?' I asked, as I tried to describe my previous night's visitor.

The nurse looked puzzled. 'There's no one like that here,' she said. 'You must have been dreaming.'

Had I? I wondered. Was it a dream or was it a visit from an angel – or even the remnant of my trip coming back? Whatever had happened, I felt better.

My anger had dissipated.

That day I put into practice what my visitor had told me. I smiled, said good morning to the nurses, ate all my breakfast, and when I had my session with Peter, I apologized and told him that I had been rude because I was scared.

I admitted to taking drugs, over a longer time than I had previously said. I told him I was determined to put that behind me. And hoping he would believe it, I said the drugs had made my five-year-old self appear.

I also admitted to having done a bit of shoplifting. 'Just small things from Woolworths,' I said. 'I'd never steal from a person.'

Yes, I was sorry, I assured him.

Four weeks after I had been brought into hospital, they discharged me. Medication and my agreement to turn over a new leaf would work, they said. They wanted to see me once a week. 'Just to monitor your progress,' Peter told me.

To see into my mind, I thought, but I would have agreed to anything in order to leave that place.

For a while, I was careful. I didn't stay out late, even when I was at my uncle's house. I was polite to my parents. I found new hiding-places for any drugs I bought. A plastic bag dug into the ground was one, but I kept to just a few joints. That five-year-old scared me.

For a year it worked – until they found out about my prostitution.

41

I hadn't meant to start taking drugs again. I hadn't planned to seek out those men – the ones I knew would pay for sex. But, like a magnet, the friends I had made before I went into the hospital drew me back in. To begin with it was just a shared joint passed around, but within a matter of weeks I was taking Mandies again. Then there was the request for me to pay my share. Nothing in the world was free, I had learnt, but where was I to get the money from?

My parents, having no knowledge of how I had paid for the drugs my mother had found, were stricter with my pocket money. A limited budget would stop me purchasing them again, they thought. If I told them there was something I wanted, they demanded proof that that was what I had purchased with the money they had given me. So they were not an option.

Even though my mother had told him not to give me any, I knew I could inveigle cash out of my uncle; but somehow I no longer wanted to. Wheedling meant being friendly to him, and I found that increasingly difficult.

So I found those men again. Occasionally I made a mistake and was turned down with a disapproving, knowing look that made me cringe, but mainly I wasn't. With the money came a sense of freedom. I had my independence again and could buy what I wanted. But I was still careful. For a while I was complacent in my belief that I had been careful enough not to get caught, that my drug-taking was under control, that the teachers put my lack of concentration down to the time I had spent in hospital and that no one suspected a thing. I soon had a rude awakening.

It was a teacher I'd had more than one run-in with who told me I was to go to the headmistress's study. As she said those words, I felt a vague tightening in my gut. It was the beginning of fear. Somehow I knew that at least some of my activities had come to light. Her next words confirmed that my fear was far from groundless.

'You've been found out, Jackie. Mind you, I've always known what a little slut you are.' Her thin lips stretched into a sneer and the triumphant expression on her face told me that someone had talked. I wondered who it had been – not one of the men who wanted sex with an under-age girl, I was sure.

As though she had guessed my thoughts, the teacher answered my silent question. 'Not every man you propositioned said yes, did he? Remember the one who told you not to be a silly little girl and you answered him by saying you had plenty of experience. Well, his daughter goes to school here. He described you, Jackie, and guess what – she knew who you were, all right. And knew your reputation – it seems half the school does.'

My heart sank. I remembered that man. He was someone I had seen with one of my punters, so I'd thought he would be all right. Shit. Clearly not.

At her revelations that vague feeling of fear turned into an icy lump that chilled me and brought gooseflesh to my arms. This, I knew, was not going to be something I could talk myself out of.

'You'll never come to anything,' she said. 'You'll just end up on the streets. See if you don't. A common little whore, that's what you are, and that's what you'll always be.'

On and on she went as she walked beside me down those long corridors that led to the headmistress's study – how it was my parents she felt sorry for, how I'd always been trouble, how the school should have got rid of me years ago. I blocked her words out. She was enjoying this, I thought, as I kept my head up and tried to ignore her.

She hadn't enough imagination to think of fresh insults to hurl at me so she repeated the earlier one: 'Just a common little whore, that's what you are,' she hissed.

At that I felt a mist of rage descend. What did she know, the ugly cow? I thought angrily. 'What's the matter? Found out your boyfriend's one of the ones I've been with?' I snapped.

She gripped the top of my arm hard and laughed. 'He's got better taste, Jackie.'

'Yeah,' I said. 'That's what all the wives and girlfriends think.'

A red tide suffused her cheeks and she propelled me into the headmistress's office without a further word.

'She's admitted it and not a scrap of shame either,' she said, as she entered the room.

The expression on the headmistress's face was neither triumphant nor sneering. Her face showed no pleasure at having caught me out in something that the school would not be able to tolerate. Instead, she just looked incredibly sad. She dismissed the teacher, who almost flounced out of the room in her disappointment at not being a witness to my final half-hour at the school. The headmistress told me to take a seat, as she had wanted to speak to me in private.

'I remember you when you first came here, Jackie. You were a troubled little girl even then,' she said, more with some remnant of affection than anything else.

I, too, remembered those early days. A picture of the panic attack I had had on my first day at school when her voice had reassured me that I was going to be all right and that I was safe came into my mind. I saw her face as it had been that day, concerned, not angry as I had expected.

For the first time I felt a wave of shame at what I had done and, unable to meet her eyes, I looked away.

I knew that whatever I said or however sorry she felt for me, now that she knew what I had been doing it was impossible for her to keep me at the school. With that realization, I wanted to be a small child again, to rest my head on her shoulder as I had after that panic attack, and to be told that everything was going to be all right. But there was no turning back and I had to accept the consequences of my actions.

I was right. She said that they had tried to help me but in her opinion I needed more than the school could give. Therefore it was no longer the right environment for someone with my problems.

I'll corrupt the other children is really what she means, I thought.

'I suppose you did it to finance your drug habit,' she said. 'Yes, Jackie, I know about that,' she added, when she saw the surprise on my face. I did not answer her, for what was there to say? If she knew about that, then I was sure my parents did as well.

She had already spoken to them about her decision, she said, as though she had read my mind. They were already at the school and were going to take me home. She told me she was sorry that somehow the school had failed me, that she knew I had problems. Then she repeated what she had already said: that I needed a special type of care that she and the school were unable to provide.

She wished me luck and hoped I would sort myself out.

I would have preferred her to be angry, even to have said the same words the teacher had. Her sadness and disappointment hurt much more than those harsh words had.

I wanted to say something, anything, to show that I, too, was sorry, but the words stayed in my throat.

'Come, Jackie,' she said, 'your parents are waiting outside. I'll walk you out.' She touched my arm briefly as I went through the doors. 'Goodbye, Jackie,' she said, but I was too emotional to reply and, without a backward glance, I walked through the gates to where my stony-faced parents were waiting in their car. Still silent, I climbed in.

42

Once back at the house, after she had venomously told me how I had shamed her and that I was a filthy little girl whom she wanted nothing more to do with, my mother refused to speak to me.

My father at first demanded the names of the men I had been with. I told him I had never asked. 'I could go to the police,' he said. 'They've committed a crime.'

'Well, it wasn't rape, was it?' I said defiantly.

'No publicity,' screamed my mother, no doubt imagining headlines splashed across the newspapers, exposing the debauchery within the middle classes.

'How many, Jackie?' my father whispered angrily, when my mother was out of earshot.

I looked at him with pity then. 'More than you want to know,' I said.

'It hasn't just started, has it?' he said tiredly. 'You were selling yourself to get money for drugs before you went into hospital, weren't you?'

I saw his shoulders slump when I answered him with just one word, 'Yes.'

'Why?' he asked, but that was something I couldn't answer.

I was banished to my room. Meals were placed outside my door; a curt knock announced their arrival. For the following week not only did my mother not speak to me, she refused to acknowledge my existence.

At the end of my week's banishment, I was told to come downstairs as they wanted to talk to me. My parents explained what had been arranged. I was being sent to a school that catered for problem children. I was to pack suitable clothing and be ready to leave in the morning.

'It's where I wanted you to go to before you were admitted to hospital,' my mother told me. 'It was your father who insisted on us giving you more support. Well, that's backfired on him, hasn't it?'

Those, I think, were the last words my mother spoke to me for several years.

The next morning, true to their word, they drove me to the school where I was to board. My parents had been right: it was a place for disturbed children. They had been taken to the school to stay there until they were considered old enough to fend for themselves. In some cases their parents, unable to cope with their children's behaviour, had left them to the care of the professionals, while others had been removed from their homes by Social Services.

'That,' I said to my therapist, 'is the end of the second part of my story and the beginning of the third. Maybe underneath,' I reflected, 'I wanted my parents to say that, no matter what I had done, they loved me, that they would help me, that there had to be a reason for my actions. But no. All my mother cared about was her reputation. And my father, well, he was just angry with the men who had paid me for sex. But did he try and go to the police? He was right. What those men had done with me might not have been rape but it was a criminal act. I was under age and, at twelve, I in no way looked sixteen. So they couldn't have used the defence that they hadn't realized how young I was. In fact, they couldn't have in the year after I came out of hospital either. Even with makeup on, I still looked young. After all, that was what they'd liked, wasn't it? No, he just shouted and blustered at first, then got upset, but in the end he agreed with my mother, that it was pointless trying to bring charges. Instead I was to be sent away.

'That was the . . .' I searched for the right word.

'The catalyst, maybe?' said my therapist, helpfully.

'Yes, that's it – the catalyst for what happened next and the real beginning of the third part of my story. I knew my parents, the school, my classmates – everyone – thought I was bad and, like people do, I saw myself through their eyes and believed I was. I'm not proud of everything that happened next. It was, after all, of my own making,' and, faltering, for the next part was still painful, I started to tell her what the next few years had brought.

43

It was at that school that I decided I was never going home. If my parents had washed their hands of me, then I had washed mine of them. I did not want to see my parents or my uncle or any of the people my parents socialized with. I was sure that everyone knew what I had done, even Kat. I knew if I ever returned to that area I would be a pariah, someone at whom fingers would be pointed before backs were turned. I couldn't face that.

The people running the school were nice enough – I can still see the head: she reminded me of a fat pigeon. She was somewhere in her forties, I would think, a short woman with a formidable bust. However hard she tried to hide it under baggy jumpers and shirts, it still jutted out aggressively, and her equally large behind was encased in tight grey trousers.

But her bark was worse than her bite. She believed in us learning self-discipline, rather than being told what to do every minute.

'Now, Jackie,' she had said, on my first day there, 'we do have a few rules,' and she informed me that class attendance was compulsory, then outlined when we would have meals and free time. 'But,' she added, 'this is not a prison. We believe that you have to set your own boundaries.' She went on to tell me that at weekends we were allowed into town, that we didn't have to wear uniform, and should we feel the need to talk, there was always someone on hand to listen.

Wow! I thought. This is better than I expected.

For the first few days I tried to find my feet, kept my head down and turned up promptly for all my classes. Each morning when I woke it took me a few seconds to realize where I was. There was none of the birdsong I had always heard through my bedroom window at home. It couldn't penetrate the thick walls of the building. Neither could I hear cars revving, as I had when my father and some of the other men on our estate left for work. My mother's voice didn't call me to get up. Instead the harsh ring of a bell roused me, the bell that told everyone that there was just three-quarters of an hour before we were expected to be in the dining room for breakfast.

Just forty-five minutes to get into the shower, brush my teeth and dress. With that thought, instead of flopping back on to my pillow, I would swing my legs out of the bed and rush to one of the bathrooms.

Four of us shared that room – two sisters and a girl who, like me, had been placed there by her family. The sisters, whose single mother apparently showed little inter-est in either their well-being or their whereabouts, had been disruptive at school when they had turned up for classes instead of playing truant. Like me, they had taken drugs and rebelled against authority, but unlike me they had broken into a pensioner's home and stolen money.

They should have been taken to court, but Social Services had argued that their bad home environment had turned them into youthful criminals. No charge had been brought against them; instead, they had been placed in the school.

The other girl was a small, angry person. Her stepfather had never left her alone, she had told us. He had been forever touching her. One day her mother had walked into the kitchen when she was fending off yet another pass. Her mother had accused her of trying to seduce her new husband. No matter what her daughter said in her defence, she was not believed.

'She knew what he was up to all right, the filthy bastard,' she said. 'Just suited her to call me a liar instead of kicking him out. She went at me, you know, screaming and shouting. Her face was right in mine – I could feel her spit landing on my cheeks.'

'So what got you in here?' I asked.

'The knife did. I went for him the next time he tried it on – sliced his arm.' Her face lit up at the memory. 'Oh, he told her I'd lost it. That I was jealous, that it was me who had tried it on with him. He said that when he'd pushed me away, I'd gone for him. So they put me in here. Stupid bitch, my mother is. He only married her for her money. When my dad died, he left plenty of life insurance, and what did the fucking grieving widow do? Took herself off to those singles clubs, shagged her arse off with the low-life men she picked up in them, then met that fucking bastard and married him. She's ten years older than him and looks it, even if she does prance around in tight clothes and bleach her hair blonde. But she believes he loves her. Wouldn't listen to a word I said, just called me a pathetic little whore. Anyhow, I'm finished with her.'

'Bleeding hell,' said one of the sisters, when she heard that story. 'How stupid can women be?'

Pretty stupid, I thought, remembering some of the

black eyes I'd seen on the council estate and how those women had refused to bring charges against the men who had beaten them.

It didn't take me long to meet the rest of the teenagers who were in the school. Damaged children every one of them. They had all – somewhere, somehow – been let down by the adult world. Once, maybe when they were little, with some degree of trust left, they could have been saved – saved from the beatings, the neglect and the abuse that had made them unruly and hard. Maybe if they had been taken away and loved enough they might have grown into happy teenagers. But that was not what had happened to that bunch of feral-eyed children. By the time they were placed in the school, it was far too late to help them. They saw adults as the enemy and the place they were in, however lenient, as a prison.

They came from all walks of life. Some were from impoverished areas but others, like me, had come from a home where lack of money was not the problem. Some had been born into dysfunctional families and had grown up hearing drunken rows for as long as they could remember. Having been carelessly disciplined, given meals sporadically and sent to school unwashed, they had run wild and rebelled against any type of discipline. Eventually when their school and their parents had had enough of them, they were sent to a place where they could have professional care. The bodies of others bore the scars and marks of old beatings and they wore their anger like a banner.

The ones I thought had suffered most were the quiet ones. With their arms wrapped around their bodies, they looked out at the world through eyes from which the innocence of childhood had long gone. Some were so disturbed that foster home after foster home had given up on them and returned them to the state's care.

But however they had come to be in that school, they all had one thing in common: they felt worthless.

There was one boy, the eldest of six children, who was angry and bitter at the system he thought had let him down. 'Don't think my mother knew who half our fathers were,' he said offhandedly, as though that was normal. 'But you know, in her own way, she tried. Well, when she was sober she did. The neighbours kept reporting her about the state we were all in, how the baby cried all day, the men she brought home, and the screaming rows that the whole neighbourhood could hear. Round those do-gooders would come. I'd see their faces grimacing at the state of our home – she never cleaned it. There would be empty booze bottles all over the place. But they never took us away, not even when they could see my baby brother was stuck in the same stinking nappies all day. Funny thing, though – the dog. We'd gone on, as kids do, that we wanted one. In the end she said I could have a puppy for my birthday. Off we all went to one of those homes where strays were being looked after. They had nice clean cages and plenty of food. Lucky them, I thought. The ads said they needed new homes. I picked one little black-and-white thing up. It licked my nose and I decided that was the one for me. And you know what those people that worked there said then?'

'No,' I said.

'That we had to fill in a form and answer loads of questions. Like would someone be in all day – they didn't want to think of a puppy being left. And did we have a garden? My mum said there was a park and she didn't go out to work so it would have company, if that was what bothered them. I think it was the sight of all us that worried them. A bunch of scruffy kids, the baby in a beat-up pushchair, and even though she'd cleaned herself up, my mum still looked a mess. But they didn't say that. They just told us that someone would call round and see us all at home.

'Well, this lady arrived, unexpected, like. Well, you should have seen her face when my mum let her in – she'd been drinking as usual and smelt like a brewery. That lady couldn't wait to leave and we never got the dog. Our house wasn't suitable, they said. I thought it funny that it was all right for us kids to stay there, but not good enough for a little mongrel dog.' He laughed harshly.

'So how did you end up here?' I asked.

'She got a new man who beat us up when he was drunk. Put the little 'un in hospital, the bastard. The police were called and brought in Social Services, who took us away. We were all sent to different foster homes. But the one I went to didn't want me, so I got sent here.'

'And your mother?' I asked.

'She can fuck off,' he said. 'Stupid cow, she took him back, you know, after what he did.'

He was just one who spat with rage when he talked about his parents. When questioned, I said I had played truant, hung around with the wrong friends, done drugs and got caught.

'Is that all?' they asked.

Well, it was all I was going to admit to.

Pocket money was limited in the school. Instead, we were given odd jobs where we were rewarded with small amounts of extra cash. Earning money was meant to give us self-respect, I was told.

Not bloody likely, was the sentiment many of us expressed. We did the odd chore so as not to raise suspicion and then, like the teenagers I had met before, looked for other ways to supplement our incomes.

We would take a bus to the next town, pair up and shoplift. We sold the stuff – tapes, small items of clothing, makeup, perfume – to contacts that those who had been in the school for several months had made. Marijuana was bought, joints rolled and passed round and, for a while, I thought little had changed for me.

My five-year-old self came out a couple of times, but without the pressure of being in my parents' house, she seemed happier, or so I was told. Well, she didn't throw herself at a wall. And the matron seemed able to cope with her.

44

I stayed there for several months. When the first holiday came round, then the second, my parents refused to have me at home. I, like some of the other children, remained at the school. Christmas came and went. Then it was Easter and my parents finally agreed that I could go home for a week.

The headmistress called me to her office and imparted the news in the expectation that I would be overjoyed at the thawing of my parents' resolve to have nothing to do with me.

I wasn't. Their minds might have changed, but mine had not. I had no intention of seeing my parents again, and it was then that I decided to leave.

Dave had managed to get up to see me a few times – we had met in town – and it was him that, in a panic, I had phoned. He had moved away from his parents and gone to London while I had been at the school. It was to there that I made arrangements to go.

I waited till the weekend when we were free to go into town, threw as much of my stuff into a duffel bag as I could and simply walked out.

I don't think my parents would have opted for that place if they had known how easy it was to leave and how little supervision there was. Before anyone could realize I was missing, I was on the train.

Dave and I had decided that with the coach taking six hours, even though it was cheaper, catching it was risky. I might be stopped once I reached London. Once the school reported that a girl was missing the coach station would be the first place the police would go to make enquiries. I bought a ticket to Manchester, changed there and bought another to London. That'll throw them off the scent, I thought. They'll think I'm on my way home and it'll give me more time to travel without being detected.

That day, I felt I was having the biggest adventure of my life. I sat in a smoking compartment and sipped coffee. I hadn't dared to try to buy wine or beer from the bar. Not seeing anyone who looked the least bit interested in me, I lit cigarette after cigarette and placed my headphones on my head. Won't be long before I'm smoking something a bit more interesting than this, I thought. Then, pressing my forehead against the window, I watched as the train flashed past small towns and villages. It was when we got to the outskirts of London that I began to see just how big it was. Rows and rows of terrace houses and council estates of old brick tenement buildings where I could see washing hanging out on the balconies, then the more modern tower blocks with their high windows and nearby play areas.

It was early evening when the train drew into Euston and, picking up my bag, I jumped on to the platform ready for the next stage of my adventure.

As I gave my ticket to the inspector and walked through the barrier, I was oblivious to everyone except Dave, who was standing there with a huge grin on his face. He gave me an enveloping hug, took my bag and led me to the escalators that descended to the Underground.

I stood on the moving staircase as it took me down and down. I could feel people jostling me, but it was the noise I was conscious of: the roar of the trains, the loudspeaker announcing arrivals, the warning to mind the gap, and the hundreds of commuters rushing to their platforms.

Once on the crowded train, we had to stand with my bag between Dave's feet. Hanging on to an overhead strap, I swayed backwards and forwards in time to the train's movements. I found it hard to keep my balance as it charged through the tunnel before it stopped to let a few people off and still more on.

We changed from the Northern Line, which Dave told me was the oldest section of the Underground, to the District Line at a station called Embankment. Again we had to stand until we reached Earl's Court, where Dave was living.

We walked down Earl's Court Road, which was full of shops that were still open and restaurants that were already full. I could hear the babble of different languages as I stared around me with something like amazement. I had visited Manchester but only in the daytime. This was the first time I had seen a city during the evening. In the area where my parents lived and the small town where my uncle's house was, all the shops were closed by five thirty. Apart from those going to the pubs or restaurants, there were very few people on the streets. Not so in Earl's Court, where the pavements were crowded. There were women dressed in saris, men wearing turbans, olive-skinned people from the Middle East, some in Western clothes, others wearing the long white *dishdasha* with, incongruously, feet in black lace-up shoes peeping out at the bottom.

I could see only the eyes and hands of their female

companions, who were wearing the *hijab* – the long, loose garment that hides the body and covers the head. In some cases even their noses were concealed by something that reminded me of a large bird's beak.

We turned left into a tree-lined street where there were four-storey houses with flaking stucco façades. Their shabbiness and the rows of bells by the front doors showed that it had been many years since they were one residence.

'Here's where I live,' said Dave, pointing to an iron staircase that led down to a basement. Once we were in, he showed me proudly round what seemed to me a small space. My room, which had a door that led out to a tiny back yard, had been freshly painted and on the single bed there was a pretty flowery duvet cover. 'Tried to make it look nice for you,' Dave said. I smiled my appreciation.

There was no sitting room. He explained that rents were high in London, but there were a couple of chairs and an old television on the table in the kitchen so we could sit in there. Apart from that, the only other furniture was a gas stove and a fridge, both of which had seen better days.

For a moment I thought of my bedroom at my parents' house, with its fresh paint, my music, those fitted wardrobes full of clothes and, more than anything else, its cleanliness. I forced the thought away. They had sent me to that school, hadn't they? Wanted rid of me, looked at me with contempt. No, that was not my home any more. As soon as I can earn some money, I thought, I can make this place look more homely.

That night we wandered round Earl's Court, ate a curry at a small restaurant and went for a drink in a noisy bar. 'You sit down,' Dave told me, guiding me to a dim corner.

'Don't want anyone noticing that you look a bit young.' But no one paid me any attention.

For the first few weeks, London was fun. I tried to find work, even though Dave had told me he earned enough for both of us. When he saw that I was determined to pay my own way, he suggested I tried some of the takeaway cafés in the area. They might take me on as casual labour and pay cash. But every place I went to wanted papers that showed my National Insurance number.

A couple of the owners looked at me suspiciously and asked how old I was. That scared me: I was a runaway and surely people must be looking for me. I knew my parents would have been informed that I was missing on the day I'd caught the train to Manchester. They might not want me at home, but that didn't mean they would be content for me to disappear. And I didn't want to be found. The police would have been notified, I was sure, and each time I saw a policeman or a panda car, I was nervous. I didn't know then just how many runaways end up in London and that there was a limit on the amount of police time that could be spent on tracing them.

'Just give them a false name and another address,' Dave said, when I confessed my fears to him. So, summoning up my courage, I persevered and my days took on a routine. In the mornings I ventured out, looking for work. Once or twice I was given a few hours' washing-up or clearing tables, but no would give me more than that. Not allowed, they told me, not unless I had that bloody number.

Dave kept telling me it didn't matter, but still I felt bad about it.

In the evenings, arm in arm, we ambled down the

streets to a cheap pizza place, a bar or pub. Although it was early April, it was still cold and the lights from the street lamps, cars and buses threw an orange glow over the pavements and shops. However late it was, the streets were never dark.

I liked that. Dave did 'business' from around nine. There was a pub, large, dark and dingy, its walls painted nicotine yellow. Here, hirsute men with tattoos, clad in black leather and chains, surreptitiously passed him money in exchange for small packets.

There were nights when we went to the many clubs in the area. Sometimes we did not go in, but dived into an alley where packets of white powder were exchanged for money. Once the deal was done those boys, wearing hooded jackets and new Nike trainers, slunk off into the darkness.

By midnight, Dave's pocket was bulging with money. 'Told you it doesn't matter you not working,' he said.

At the clubs, we were ushered in quickly without paying, instead of having to join a long queue. Dave, I soon learnt, knew a lot of people, and when I was looked at curiously, he told them I was his kid sister. 'Easier that way,' he said. 'Stops the questions.' Afterwards we went back to the flat to smoke thick joints, and at night my sleep was dreamless.

Saturday nights were different. Then we hailed taxis that reeked of cigarettes and warm leather and went to the West End. Dave explained that on Saturday nights promoters often took over a club and put their own staff and DJs in. Raves, they were called, and they ran for twelve hours.

I had never seen anything like it – dim lights, red walls,

black floor, sweat glistening on the bodies of the whirling, jumping, spinning youngsters with their bottles of water clutched firmly in their hands. The building seemed to vibrate with the mechanical sounds of the music that Dave told me was a combination of house and techno. 'It's great,' he said. 'You can only listen to it for so long without drugs, so it's good for business.'

'I supply the dealers in here,' he told me. 'Safer that way – only they know who I am.' 'E', I learnt, was the name of the pills that were popular at the raves.

'Keeps them awake all night,' Dave said, but when I asked for one, he categorically refused. 'Stick to nice mellow dope, Jackie,' he told me sternly, each time I asked.

I personally thought he was overdoing the kid-sister bit, but decided to leave it alone.

Those Saturday nights we were out until the early hours. Then it was back to Earl's Court, where we consumed a late-night or early-morning greasy hamburger from one of those places that never seemed to shut.

On Sundays we slept late before making breakfast. Then, as I lolled around in an oversized T-shirt drinking coffee, I could hear the squeals of children playing and music – rap, pop or even the background jingle of commercials – coming from other flats and smell the aroma of different foods, curry, frying fish and others I didn't recognize, that wafted through my window. By summer I felt I belonged to this place where people from faraway countries and different parts of Britain had, for whatever reason, made their home.

45

Dave and I went to bed together just once. How can I describe that time? It was – well, what can I say? Sweet. His body was smooth, his chest free of hair. His legs entwined with mine while his hands stroked me gently; warm hands that made me feel safe. I still remember kissing his neck, that soft place just behind his ear. But he never got an erection.

'Dave, it doesn't matter,' I said and, truthfully, it didn't. 'It's just nice to be held.'

But he, of course, saw it as a failure, and refused to try again.

When it was cold, as English summers often are, we would walk under a leaden sky, oblivious to either wind or rain, my hand tucked into his pocket, his fingers over mine. When we went for a drink I would sit as close to him as I could and, in the midst of other people, my head would rest on his shoulder.

When I went to bed he would kiss me on the cheek and say goodnight, and when he thought I was asleep I would hear him leave. He believed he had fooled me, but I knew every time.

There were mornings when he couldn't meet my eyes and I would chatter brightly so as not to face him with his deception.

Oh, I wanted him to stay in, to come to my bedroom again. I wanted it to be all right.

'You loved him?' my therapist asked.

'Yes,' I said. 'I loved him. He was the only man I ever did love.'

Then there was the night he came back very drunk and his stumbling around the flat woke me. I got out of bed, walked into his room and turned the light on.

He put his hand up to shield his eyes from the sudden glow, stood there swaying slightly, and I saw he was crying. 'Dave, where have you been?' I asked. Afterwards I thought it was strange that I asked that, not what the matter was. I reached up to his shoulders, pressed them slightly till he finally sank down on the bed. Then I saw the blood. Splashes of it were all over his T-shirt, and when I lifted his hand, I saw the knuckles were raw. There were scratches on his face, a bruise by his eye and I knew something bad had happened.

He told me then where he went at night.

It was to the bars, the ones where leather-clad men with hot, hungry eyes went in search of sex. There would be a dark back room where they went with partners they wouldn't have recognized in the light. They were not men who wanted to share a drink and talk before going back to a flat and calling what happened next lovemaking, as though that was possible with someone unknown. They wanted nameless sex in the dark with complete strangers.

'There was a boy in the bar,' he said. 'He was different. He didn't want to go to the back room, he wanted to talk. He had blond hair and the most amazing green eyes. Nicky, he said his name was. I went with him, went back to his flat.'

'And?' I asked.

'We fucked. He said it was special for him. That I was different and that he wanted to see me again. I wanted him to stop talking, to just let me leave, but he tried to stop me and then it happened.'

'What, Dave?' I asked. 'What happened?'

'I hit him. It was seeing that pleading look on his face that did it. He was beautiful and I wanted to hurt him. To take away that look of innocence. How could I – how could I have let him do what my father did to me, Jackie? How could I have enjoyed it? I hurt him,' he said, 'broke his nose, worse maybe, and I left him there.'

I put my arms round Dave and held him as he sobbed for the boy Nicky and the boy he himself had once been.

I was only fifteen but I felt old, so old. I wanted to tell him that everything would be all right, but I knew that nothing was going to be all right again. Instead I made him take his shoes off and get on to the bed. Then I lay beside him. I pressed myself close against his body until my breath mingled with his. Our eyes held each other's until he reached over and turned off the light. That night in patches of silence, in wordless darkness, we spoke to each other without uttering a sound, of pain, bewilderment and hurt.

As the dark of night gave way to the violet shadows of dawn, we fell asleep. He was heavy against my arm but I didn't move. I wanted his weight pressed against me and his breath on my face. I wanted to be the first thing he saw when he woke.

He left me. He was frightened the police would look for him, frightened of what he had done but, more than any-thing, frightened of himself.

'Go home, Jackie,' he said, when I begged him to take me with him. 'Don't you see what I am?'

But I only saw Dave, the boy I loved.

'You're not safe with me any longer.'

'Why?' I asked.

'Because.' His hand ran through my hair, wound some strands around it and tightened. 'I seem to want to hurt whoever loves me.' I felt the strength of his fingers.

He gave me money, enough to take me back to my parents. 'They'll look after you,' he said. 'You're not bad like me, just fucked up a bit. Tell them you need help, tell them the truth. But go back.'

I said I would, not because I meant it but because I wanted to please him.

He left that day and my heart broke. That was when I wanted to cry, to shake with sobs and be soaked with anguish, but even then I was still unable to shed a tear. Instead I burnt myself. I used candles and the lighter, bit down hard on my lip till the blood poured between my teeth, cut underneath my foot, but nothing stilled my inner pain.

'Did you hear from him again?' asked my therapist.

'Yes,' I said, 'I did, but not until the end of the next part of my story.'

'And you saw him again?'

'Just once,' I said.

When the landlord realized I was in the flat on my own, he told me that I had to get out. I knew that Dave had paid a deposit and, again summoning up my courage, I asked for it.

'It's not yours, is it, girlie?' he said, and laughed in my face. 'When Dave comes and asks, I'll give it to him. Less damages, of course,' he added, looking round the flat with a sneer. I knew that he knew that that was not going to happen.

He stood over me while I threw into my bag as many of my possessions as would fit into it. Then he put his hand out for the key. I did not know that he was breaking the law by making me leave in that manner. Even if I had, I would have been too scared to protest, so I just left.

I had the money Dave had given me, which I thought would buy me time. I tried the YWCA. It was full. I went to a small bed-and-breakfast where the manager, seeing my youth and that the only luggage I had was a scruffy duffel bag, demanded money up front. It was too much, more than I could afford. I said I'd come back later and, clutching my bag, I wandered into the streets. I knew that trying to find a room was hopeless: however much makeup I plastered on, however hard I tried to look confident, no landlord would rent to me. Not only did I not have proof that I was old enough to live away from home, I did not have enough funds to pay a month's rent plus a deposit.

I must have walked miles that day – walked until I reached an area where there was only one doorbell on the large houses. Then I passed red-brick mansion blocks of flats and eventually came to Harrods, the huge department store. After gazing at the magnificent window displays, I continued walking towards the West End. I went with little purpose and no plan of what I was going to do next. Before I knew it, I was in Piccadilly Circus. It was then, knowing I had become one of them, that I really saw the homeless.

Some were huddled in sleeping-bags, for the chill of autumn was in the air, with a cap or a piece of cardboard lying in front of them as they begged for money.

A girl, not much older than me, dressed in a thin denim jacket and patched jeans, crouched in a doorway. Long, greasy hair partially obscured a pallid face as, with eyes cast down, her shaking fingers rolled a thin cigarette. A few coins lay on a plastic plate beside her, to give further encouragement to passers-by. Without looking up, she repeated over and over her refrain, 'Spare any change,' to every pair of legs she saw.

'Help with food for my dog,' was the next plaintive request from a youth wearing a khaki combat jacket and army-style boots. His faithful friend, a placid brindled Lurcher, whose large head rested on outstretched paws, lay on a grubby blanket by his master's side, paying little heed to his surroundings.

Prancing on the pavement inches away from them, a small white dog, wearing a diamanté leather collar and a doggy 'designer' sheepskin jacket, stopped, cocked one leg against a nearby lamp post, then continued walking. His owner, a woman in her early twenties, her long, streaked blonde hair flying and high-heeled boots clicking, clutched his lead tighter in her gloved hand and looked straight ahead.

London, a city of contrasts: to that woman, the homeless were invisible, anonymous, annoying whiny voices coming out of the shadows of doorways.

I went to a camping shop, bought a sleeping-bag, dark blue with a bright yellow lining. That night, too frightened to sleep, I sat in a doorway with my legs against my chest and my arms tucked into the bag. Hidden at the bottom of it were my purse and my few possessions.

That was when I thought I had hit rock bottom.

*

For my first few days on the streets, I was clean enough not to look destitute. I went to coffee shops, with my sleeping-bag wrapped in the bag it had come in. I used their amenities to wash my face and brush my teeth. But gradually the dirt of the streets clung to me and, with it, the acrid smell of the homeless.

Unless someone has slept on the streets, it is impossible to visualize the dehumanization it brings. We spent nights quivering with fear lest our few goods were stolen or even worse that we were murdered or raped. In the morning, the sound of traffic woke us and we could hear voices and footsteps of people walking past – past us, the invisible people.

It was a week before I, too, whined from a doorway, 'Spare any change?' then seized the coins dropped on to my piece of cardboard. My hair became lank; grime crept under my nails and into the creases of my hands and neck. Now the smart coffee shops barred my entrance. 'You can't come in here,' they said. To them I had ceased to be a person – I was just an unsightly something that they did not want on their premises.

I moved around, as we all did in our search for sites where the people were generous. Shaftesbury Avenue, with its theatres, restaurants and bars, was where I headed at night. There, people flocked from the theatres or pubs, faces flushed with bonhomie.

'Spare any change?' I said, time and again, and as my voice scratched irritatingly on the edge of their consciousness, coins were tossed down carelessly before the man or woman climbed into a taxi that would take them back to their centrally heated home.

The worst were the ones who thought they had a duty to lecture me.

'I don't give money,' they said self-righteously. 'You should get a job.'

But by then I had learnt how hard it was for the homeless to achieve that. We had no address to give and nowhere to make ourselves look presentable. Social Services would not pay out to people without accommodation, and even if they had, I was still under age and a runaway.

Over the weeks, I blended in with the vast invisible army of the homeless and met others who, like me, had run away. Young and broken, they had escaped from bullying stepfathers, drunken parents who beat them, foster families who abused them and children's homes that had failed them. Everyone had a story – and few seemed to think it would ever have a happy ending.

I found a certain comradeship. Sometimes it was just the sharing of a doorway, being shown where the best café was for a cheap breakfast, and taken to the places where at night volunteers came round with free food.

We tried to avoid the older ones who, shapeless in their bundles of tattered clothing, stank of cheap alcohol, bad teeth and unwashed bodies.

Passers-by recoiled from them as, pushing their stolen shopping trolleys filled with plastic bags that contained all they thought was precious, they muttered, swore and shook their fists at demons only visible to themselves.

Unable to gain admittance to even the scruffiest of cafés, they had no other recourse than to find a bush in one of the parks or a dark alleyway to relieve themselves. I once saw a deranged old lady lift her skirts and squat in the middle of the road. The cars just swerved round her. Had she come into the world so alone that there was no one, no relative, who could have cared for her? 'Where have they all come from?' I asked a boy, after I'd witnessed that incident.

'They were kicked out of the mental hospitals when Mrs Thatcher closed them down,' he told me. 'She said the community would care for them, but the fucking community doesn't want to know. Does it?' And it appeared that they didn't.

It was cold that winter and we searched for sheltered places and doorways deep enough to protect us from the lashing rain. I discovered that at night, when the temperature dropped, cold water was sluiced over the steps of certain restaurants to keep us away. When it froze, we would have to search out another place to sleep.

There was one restaurant where parents of small children could meet for a weekend brunch. They could hand over their warmly dressed offspring to a clown or face painter, then relax over cocktails and order food. Content that their children were being cared for, they lingered over lunch. When they left, we would stand nearby the door, hoping for some coins to come our way. They seldom did. Instead the mothers moved their children a little faster past us, no doubt frightened that our homelessness was contagious.

Incensed that we had the temerity to loiter anywhere near his premises, that particular restaurateur was proud of his actions. He didn't stop at throwing water on the steps and letting it freeze. Instead he waited for us to tuck ourselves into our sleeping-bags and huddle up together.

It was then that he turned the high-pressure hoses on us, the ones that were used to clean the streets. Jets of freezing water saturated us and all our possessions. The force was so powerful that one slight girl was thrown against the doors.

'I want to wash the vermin off the streets,' he said, roaring with laughter at the damage he had caused. Dazed and bewildered by his cruelty, we gathered up our wrecked possessions and crawled away. My treasured Walkman was destroyed that night.

There was an outcry: newspapers published his remarks and people recoiled at his heartlessness – but that didn't make any difference to the amount of money that was dropped near my hand.

After a month, I was oblivious to the smell of my body, my dirty lank hair and the grubbiness of my clothes. I was no longer concerned about how I looked. Thick jumpers too large for me, bought from charity shops, became my nightwear, the steps my bedroom, the scant public toilets, with only cold water in the taps, my bathroom – and solvents my new drugs.

Did I think of returning home? No. Did I think of a future? Maybe sometimes, for a fleeting moment. Just existing took up all my energy.

My five-year-old self, if she made an appearance, was not noticed by the human flotsam around me, so if she appeared, wondering what world she had stepped into and then left, I have no memory of it. It is doubtful that the homeless would have told me if she had. They were not critical of each other. If they had seen anything, they would most probably have put it down to an odd reaction to the glue I had sniffed and left me alone.

46

It was not just the rain and sleet that were our enemies but also the howling winds that drove it in thick sheets against our bodies. We would cover our sleeping-bags with whatever we could find – cardboard, plastic bags and pieces of matting to try and keep the worst off. But however hard we tried, the water seeped in, soaking not just us but everything we owned.

It was when rain was dripping from my hair and running down my face and my teeth were chattering with cold, my voice shaking with the effort of asking one more pair of legs for change, that I heard a voice and realized it was speaking to me.

'You look very cold,' it said.

The old me might have muttered, 'No shit,' or 'Clever bastard, aren't you?' but the rain and the cold had chased away that person. Instead, I looked up, feeling simple gratitude at the concern shown in those words.

He was young, somewhere in his middle twenties, and strikingly good-looking: tall and slim with black hair pulled back from a bony face and dark green eyes, which crinkled at the corners as he smiled down at me.

'Come,' he said. 'I'll get you a hot drink and something to eat. In a café,' he added quickly, in case I was suspicious of his intentions.

That was the night I met Eddie.

He took me to a pizza place somewhere off St Martin's Lane. A wave of hot air filled with the aroma of garlic and pizza dough greeted me as we entered.

The buzz of conversation in the crowded place, with its cheerful red-checked tablecloths and candles stuck in Chianti bottles, not to mention the thought of real food, made me relax for the first time, it seemed, in many weeks.

My jacket was removed and my damp clothes steamed in the warmth.

'Have a glass of red wine. It'll do you good, put some colour in your cheeks,' he said, pouring from a bottle that had been brought to the table.

'Choose whichever toppings you want,' he said, and I shook my head, confused at the choice – cheese, salami, chicken, seafood, artichokes. I told him to choose and that I knew any of them would taste wonderful. He ordered two thin and crispy, large, with all the extra toppings. Within minutes, a plate was in front of me.

Strings of cheese fell down my chin as, using my grubby fingers, I forgot any table manners my mother had drummed into me. My knife and fork sat untouched – it was easier to shovel pizza into my mouth with my hands. Without needing to be told again, I washed it down with large gulps of red wine.

As I ate he studied me intently and asked what had happened to me, how I had come to be on the streets. My glass was filled again, and before I knew it, I had confided in him the details of the last couple of years of my life. How I had been sent to the special school, how I had run away and ended up in London. I couldn't tell him about

Dave, just that the friend I had been staying with had left the flat where I had been living.

'What happened then?' he asked.

'The landlord came round and told me to get out.'

'What about your parents? Could you not have gone to them?'

'They don't want me,' I said, omitting to say that, if I had rung them, my father would not have turned his back on me.

'So, you have nowhere to go?' he asked. 'No friends who could help you?'

I shook my head.

'How old are you?'

'Fifteen,' I told him, and in admitting that, I had confirmed what he already thought, that I was an underage runaway.

'You're very pretty,' he said, 'too pretty to be on the streets. You're lucky to have survived so long.'

Why did no inkling of suspicion come into my head then? I think it was because he was so good-looking, and young.

He told me he had a sister my age, how he would hate it if she lived as I had. How he hoped that if anything like that ever happened to her, there would be someone out there to offer her help.

'I can give you a bed to sleep in, with clean sheets, and you can have a hot bath too, wash your clothes,' he told me. 'I want to help you.'

Well, I thought, the worst is that he might want sex.

I was wrong. That was not the worst, not nearly the worst.

He gave me dope again, nice, mellow dope.

Later he gave me something else.

He took me back to his flat that night. And, like a grateful puppy that has found a new home, I trotted along beside him.

He ran a hot bath for me, poured in something sweet-smelling and let me soak right up to my ears. There was a soft fluffy dressing-gown to snuggle up in and a big T-shirt to sleep in.

He showed me where the spare bedroom was, turned the bed down and left just the glow of the bedside lamp on.

That night, unafraid, I slept well.

In the morning he resumed the role of big brother. Breakfast was made and served to me, more concerned questions were asked, and for the first time since Dave had disappeared, I felt safe.

That was how I came to live with Eddie. Tall, good-looking, charming and empathetic Eddie, who had stored up every bit of information I had blurted out when red wine had hit an empty stomach.

I wish I had never met him.

47

Information, I learnt, but not fast enough, was money in the bank to Eddie.

I was not naïve about what sometimes happens to girls who are 'rescued' from begging in doorways. I'd seen some, who had found out that the streets of London were not paved with gold, standing shivering on street corners, waiting for a punter in a car to stop. I'd watched curiously as they climbed in and were driven away, then returned to the same spot later. Other men had picked them up in the early hours of the morning, the same ones who, once darkness fell, had brought them to the streets.

I had heard whispers about how they sold themselves, and that most of their earnings went to their pimps.

But that could never happen to me, could it? I was far too smart.

It did.

Oh, not at once – it was a gradual process that crept up on me until I found myself in a bedroom with a man I didn't know.

'You might wonder,' I said to my therapist, who had not yet shared with me anything she thought, 'what was the difference between that and what I had done in my home town. But it was different. Often the first time those men spoke to me was to tell me to take my clothes off. My body was no longer mine, but then neither was the money. It was drugs again,' I said, 'drugs that controlled me, drugs that had trapped me. Only by that time I had not stopped at smoking dope and swallowing a few Mandies.'

'Tell me about the early days first, Jackie,' was all she said, and I continued with my story.

The early days when I lived with Eddie were wonderful. The first day we went on a shopping spree, and it was like letting a child into a sweet shop, a greedy child who had gone too long without.

'Let's have a look at your clothes,' he had said earlier, then wrinkled his nose in distaste when he saw my assortment of creased, grubby garments.

He found a pair of jeans that were not too bad and a dark T-shirt. 'That,' he said, 'will have to do until we've been shopping.'

I asked how I could repay him. He said he wanted to help me and that I was not to worry. Wanting to believe him, I didn't.

'Some funky evening things first,' he said. 'I'll take you clubbing tonight.'

At the first boutique we went to he chose strappy tops in soft bright fabrics and a cropped black leather jacket.

'Skirts,' he said, when I protested that I liked jeans. Short ones that flared above my knees – and fishnet tights came next. He made me come out of the changing room and twirl round to show him each item. Like a schoolgirl, I obeyed every command while he watched me lazily. If I had known more, understood what Eddie had in mind, how he saw each purchase as an investment, I would have realized that the look he was giving me was rather like a trainer giving an untested racehorse the once-over. He was weighing me up, imagining the money he might make if I went the full distance. Maybe if I'd known that, I wouldn't have been so carefree. As it was, I didn't. I had no thoughts in my head as I handled those clothes, apart from thinking that a miracle had happened.

'Shoes,' he said, looking at my water-stained pair, and was oblivious to my protests that I really wanted another pair of Dr Martens. 'High heels,' he said, and chose a pair in black and a pair of ankle boots in soft black suede that sported four-inch stiletto heels. Then he took me to another shop where the whole ground floor seemed to be dedicated to makeup and perfume.

'Red,' he said, when my hand strayed to an orange lipstick.

Within a few minutes there was a pile of makeup and beauty products ready to be wrapped. Eddie only glanced at the bill as though it was of little importance, then peeled off more notes from his bundle and paid.

He directed me to the underwear department and stood over me, pointing to the blacks and the reds, rather than the whites and pinks. Then he took me to the final destination he had marked out for me: the hairdresser Michaeljohn near Regent Street. 'This should complete your transformation,' he said, as he left me with the stylist. 'I'll be back for you in a couple of hours.'

'Cut and streaked,' she told me, picking up my hair. Evidently Eddie had already given his instructions. The girl I had left behind, when I had taken to the streets, might have complained, but I was simply bemused by the change in my circumstances.

The stylist ran a few strands through her fingers, then told me that I needed a special conditioner.

Well, I thought, there hadn't been much chance of using one of those in a public loo.

A manicurist appeared and my broken nails were filed into shape and a glossy red polish applied before I had a chance to choose my own colour. Eddie had selected that too, it seemed.

Two hours later, I was finished. My hair, now glossy and several shades lighter, bounced on my shoulders. The street look had disappeared, all right. I just looked like a rather scruffily dressed teenager with a new hairstyle. Then I remembered all my new clothes: that look was about to change.

Eddie was waiting in Reception. He told me I looked great, tipped the stylist extravagantly, then took me for something to eat at a small wine bar where he knew the owner. It was a smart place, with pale wooden tables, chairs with cushioned seats and flower arrangements at the entrance. No questions were asked as to my age when he ordered for me, without asking, a glass of white wine and a club sandwich.

A taxi was hailed once we had finished and, surrounded by bags, I sank happily back on the seat.

In the flat I did what I had done nearly three years previously. I took out makeup and created a new me. On went the clothes and out I came, smiling with shyness and pleasure at how I knew I must look.

We went to a club that night; three large doormen stood outside and greeted Eddie as an old friend. That place, all chrome and glass, where men of all ages wore suits and girls very little, was nothing like the clubs I had visited with Dave. A long bar with a mirrored back, silver cocktail shakers, waiters in black and a small restaurant behind a glass wall made up the ground floor. Downstairs, in what must once have been a basement, there was a dance floor where a DJ mixed and spun his vinyl, while above our heads the multifaceted silver sphere rotated, sending flashes of colour down on to us.

We danced to the thumping sounds of the music, and then it was back upstairs for more drinks.

Eddie seemed to know so many of the beautiful people in the club. He took me to a room and shared a spliff with me.

'Cool,' I said, as I dragged down the smoke of the first grass I'd had for several months.

For the rest of the evening I danced, laughed, felt happy and carefree, and over the next couple of weeks little changed.

48

'A favour' was how he put it. A friend of his wanted to meet me, take me out for dinner. All I had to do was be nice. It would help him with his business – something he was rather vague about.

What could I say? He had changed my life, taken me off the streets, given me a place to stay.

That was the first time he mixed something else with the tobacco and marijuana. 'This will make you feel good,' he said, passing me the joint – and he was right. Within a few minutes, I felt as if I was cocooned in the softest of cotton wool. My whole body was completely relaxed and a sleepy euphoria swept through me. It was the most incredible buzz, far better than the strongest grass or the happy, drowsy feeling I got from Mandies.

That was my introduction to heroin.

I still felt warm and calm as he put me into a taxi and told the driver where to take me: an address in Bayswater. 'It's his flat,' he said, and told me which bell to ring.

Of course, that man and I never did go out for dinner.

There were more favours and more of something else mixed into my joints. The men were not great conversationalists – after all, there was no pretence about why I was there – but I still heard their excuses.

Going with a girl like me was not the same as being unfaithful.

'I love my wife,' most said; one even took a phone call from his and reassured her of that when he was still inside me.

49

I think if I hadn't met Gina, I would have ended up working the streets around King's Cross, desperate for my next fix. For that, I learnt, was what had happened to other girls who had had the misfortune to be 'rescued' by Eddie.

I remember so clearly the night I first saw her.

Eddie, in one of his increasingly rare spells of good humour, had taken me to a music venue in Hammersmith. We smoked joints before we left and, for once, he let me wear jeans tucked into a pair of boots and my old leather jacket – it reminded me of Dave.

There were three bands playing, but it was the last one that Eddie told me was going to be good. The drummer, obviously well known to the crowd, received a round of applause as he took his seat. His hands and feet flew as he provided a throbbing bass note below the electric guitars and the amplified voices of the band. The crowd went wild as the lead singer moved to the edge of the stage and, jumping up and down, they screamed for more after each song.

That was when I saw Gina, though I didn't know her name then. I was still buzzing with the effects of the joint and the wine that I was drinking when I saw an olive-skinned face with a wide mouth bare of makeup and dark brown hair that was almost black tumbling in thick waves to her shoulders. Her long silver earrings sparkled as, head thrown back, she laughed at something someone in her group had said. I knew I wanted to meet her. I also knew a lot more than I had the night I had met Eddie. I knew he didn't want me to have friends. Friends might put ideas into my head.

I knew it was the heroin, mixed with marijuana, that gave me the buzz I had started to crave. I knew he was a far bigger drug dealer than Dave had ever been. I knew that he had girls whose drug habit had wrecked their looks and were working the streets around King's Cross – I had met some when they had come to the flat. In some perverse way he wanted me to see them, wanted me to know what might happen, should I ever refuse what he considered was 'nice work'. That meant being sent to hotels and smart flats, rather than having to work the streets and give blow-jobs in the backs of cars. Some, like me, had once lived in his flat and catered for the 'top end of the market', as he liked to call it. But as their looks faded, they had ended up in less salubrious places.

I had learnt that Eddie did not work alone. There were the doormen, barmen and club owners he had in his pocket. He supplied drugs and girls, and they received commission on every one of their introductions. They in turn reported back when a girl got 'out of line'. He always used that term for any girl who tried to get out of his clutches or to work alone.

Getting out of line, I also learnt, ended badly.

Dave had thrashed a boy who had stolen from him, but Eddie had beaten girls who had tried to pocket more than he thought was their share of what they earned from prostitution. As far as he was concerned, he owned them. I had grown to fear Eddie. I knew I was trapped.

50

In a crowded bar it's impossible to monitor everything. While Eddie was talking to other people, I managed to get myself included in Gina's group's conversation. I found out that they were always there on a Friday night and was determined to meet up with them again. But how would I manage to do that?

My wish was granted just two weeks later. Eddie had business in Brighton. 'I'll be away for the night,' he told me.

'OK if I go to that bar and listen to some music?' I asked, trying to sound as though I didn't care either way.

He was in a good mood because he had arranged the meeting with his Brighton 'connections'. New clubs were opening there and he was setting up a dealer network to supply the drugs. He smiled and said, 'Sure,' not thinking that it might be more than music I was interested in. He peeled some notes off the wad he always had in his pocket and gave them to me. When things were going his way Eddie could be generous, but I had already seen what a bad mood could bring.

'Make sure you get the manager to order you a taxi back here,' he said. 'It can get rough round that area.' Maybe he said it out of concern but, knowing Eddie, it was more likely that he wanted to check I had gone straight home after the club closed.

When I reached the club, Gina was there with her

friends, who welcomed me with smiles. Over the evening, it became clear to me that not only did they know who Eddie was but also what he did.

'Are you his newest girl?' they asked me, not unkindly but knowingly. That was the first time I admitted to myself just what Eddie was, and what I had become.

From that night onwards, I felt a connection between Gina and myself. I loved how she laughed, how her silver bracelets jangled when she lifted her thick mane of hair off her face. More than anything I loved how, even knowing what I did, she had allowed me to join her group.

I arranged to meet her in the daytime when I managed to leave the flat on one pretext or another. Occasionally there were evenings when Eddie had no work for me and nights when he was away. The music venue seemed to be one place he didn't mind me going to on my own.

For the first time since Dave had left me, I saw what a normal life was, and I yearned to be part of it, just to be a teenager without problems. I also wanted to be with Gina more and more. At night, when I drifted off to sleep, her face came into my mind and it was her laugh that I heard ringing in my ears.

Apart from Dave, I had never had any interest in boys. Until I met Gina, I had put it down simply to not liking men, but as I thought more and more about her, I began to accept that perhaps there was another reason.

Maybe Eddie caught me daydreaming once too often or asking too frequently if I could leave the flat. Whatever the reason, he decided to tie me to him in a different way. He introduced me to the needle, showed me the buzz that came from heroin when injected straight into a vein.

He did it for me the first time, tied the strap round my arm, slapped it till the vein stood out and slid the needle in. The buzz was instant and so much more than I'd experienced when I smoked it. This was unreal. It was so beautiful and I wanted more.

The first time is always the best, I discovered, but that doesn't stop you searching for that exquisite feeling again. That's why they call it 'chasing the dragon'.

51

'You have to get away,' Gina said. 'You've got to get off the drugs, Jackie. You've seen what happens to girls who are on that stuff you're taking.

'And it's Eddie and his ilk who get them hooked. It's so they won't leave them.'

'He'd find me,' I said, and told her about other girls who had thought they could escape him. How his network had found them and the beatings they had received. Then, when they were bruised and in pain, the drugs they craved had been withheld until they had agreed to work the streets.

'He never lets them go willingly, not even when they're so low they're selling themselves for a tenner. It's a matter of principle with him. One gets away and more might leave. He'd rather see them dead.'

'Yeah, I've heard all that too,' Gina said, 'but I only half believed it.'

'Well, trust me, it's true,' I said, and felt defeated. If he could have a girl who worked the streets beaten to within an inch of her life, what would he do to me? I knew how much I was worth to him. Four or five men a week brought him in around a thousand pounds out of which he fed and clothed me, sent me to the hairdresser and gave me the odd present. Ten girls working the King's Cross area didn't earn him as much as that. Even I could work out that one docile underage girl was worth a great deal of money to him.

But, frightened as I was, Eddie had made a mistake when he had shown me the most wretched of his girls, those with dark rings round their eyes and the pallid complexion of the junkie. By doing that, he had shown me my future.

Although I'd said it wasn't a future I wanted for myself, Gina wasn't satisfied. One evening she bundled me into a taxi and made it take us to the areas where some of the street girls worked. I saw girls perhaps a couple of years older than me, standing on spindly legs that hardly appeared strong enough to support their weight. As each car passed, they looked hopefully at the driver, willing him to stop. They wore tiny mini skirts that only just covered their crotches and low-cut tops, while their feet were crammed into the highest stilettos. Nearly all of them had backcombed bleached-blonde hair, and every one of their heavily made-up faces bore the blank, dead look of someone drugged up to the eyeballs.

'Look at them, Jackie,' Gina said. 'That's your future if you don't get away. They risk their lives every time they climb into the back of a car, but do they care? No, they don't, Jackie. They only care about their next fix. And, even worse, do men like Eddie care? No. Those girls aren't people to his sort, just money. They can be replaced when they die, killed by a punter or bad drugs. But think, Jackie, not one of those girls came into this world a junkie. They were children once, and however bad their homes were, they had a future. They don't now. They'll be lucky to see their thirtieth birthdays – or unlucky depending on how you look at it.

'You might be his favourite now, but sooner or later,

he'll find some other lost soul, younger than you, get her hooked, then put her to work.

'You might last a bit longer than most. He struck lucky with you. Bet he never guessed how well you'd scrub up – but you won't last for ever. Those men he sends you to, they like change, you know. They want young innocents. They don't want the same girl every time – it takes the adventure away. Get real, Jackie. Eddie and his friends are evil bastards, and when you can't bring in the big money, he'll throw you out to work the streets with them,' she said, pointing at the sad street girls who had clearly seen better days.

She was silent then and left me to think about what she had shown me. The taxi dropped us off at a coffee shop, and once we were seated, she broached the subject of my addiction. She told me about a centre where I could get help to come off heroin and how they would prescribe other drugs, far less harmful, that would help. 'They don't expect you just to stop, you know, Jackie.'

Still I looked doubtful. Where would I go? What would I do? Eddie had controlled my life for a year, even down to what I wore and what I ate. The thought of having to make all my own decisions was suddenly very frightening.

Gina played her trump card. 'Oh, come on, Jackie! You can stay with me, if you're worried about where you'd go. I just want you to get sorted,' she said. At last I began to waver. 'And I'll take some time off work and come with you to the clinic,' she added, for good measure. She went on to tell me she had discussed it with Anna, the girl she shared her flat with, and they had agreed they wanted to help me.

'OK, then, I'll do it,' I said.

52

I was so scared the day I left Eddie, plain terrified that he might walk in and catch me. My whole body was shaking as I hastily pushed clothes and my music into plastic bags. I told Gina to wait outside in a taxi – I wanted it there ready to jump into and make a quick getaway.

I left the short skirts and skimpy tops behind. It was the jeans and T-shirts I wanted. I found some money stashed in his bedroom, about three hundred pounds. Nothing to what I had earned for him, I thought, as I shoved it into my pocket. Then, gathering everything up, I pulled on my leather jacket, raced out of the flat and jumped into the waiting cab.

The next few weeks were hard. I went to rehab, and although they prescribed methadone, coming off heroin was still worse than anything I could have imagined. I shivered and shook, sweat poured off my body and it seemed that every inch of me was racked with pain. There were so many times that I wanted to give up, find a dealer, inject the heroin into my veins and feel at peace, but then I remembered those girls with the dead eyes. Some spark of my old fighting spirit told me to persevere. Or maybe my feelings for Gina did.

The worst side effect of being drug-free was that my five-year-old self put in an appearance. It was the drugs, the doctors explained, that had kept her at bay. The methadone helped make her disappear again and, gradually, I began to feel better. I put on a little weight and started to believe that I had succeeded in turning my life around.

After I had finished my treatment I made contact with my parents. Scared they might trace the call, I had only done that once before. I felt that contacting them was part of getting well.

My mother was distant, but my father sounded excited to speak to me and wanted to know if I was all right. I told him I was clean of drugs and wanted to look for work. I had nice friends and they were helping me. 'If you need anything, I can send you money,' he said.

Had I hoped he would say, 'Just tell me where you are and I'll come and see you'? Maybe, but I consoled myself that at least he had offered me something, even if it was only money.

I loved living in Gina's flat. Anna, her flatmate, was a short, stocky girl who looked at the world myopically through thick glasses and fussed over me continuously. I could see that she had a huge crush on Gina. But she was so kind to me, I couldn't bring myself to feel jealous.

I started to wonder about looking for work. My sixteenth birthday had come and gone, which meant I was no longer an underage runaway.

My embryonic contentment made me careless. I forgot that Eddie had spies everywhere. Although we were careful not to frequent the music venue where I had first met Gina, we still went out in groups to other places where, unknown to us, there were doormen and barmen who did business with him. I don't know who told him where he could find me, but find me he did.

I was not in a bar or club when I saw him but walking down the road in broad daylight.

'Hey, Jackie,' he called.

A sick feeling of fear nearly paralysed me.

With long strides, he caught up with me. He looked calm, not angry, and somehow that terrified me even more. 'Go away,' I said, thinking that the people milling around on the street would ensure my safety.

'Don't be silly, Jackie, you're coming back with me,' he said, catching hold of my arm.

I stared at him defiantly. Surely he couldn't do anything to me in broad daylight. 'I'm not,' I answered. 'You can't make me.' I jerked my arm free and started to walk away.

But the presence of other people didn't frighten Eddie. I should have remembered what I'd once told Gina. He would rather a girl was dead than have her escape from him. I don't think I had taken more than a few steps when I felt the searing pain of the knife that was thrust deep into my back.

53

I heard Eddie's footsteps as he walked away, then the world went black.

The next thing I knew I was waking up in hospital, with no recollection of how I had got there, for the second time.

The doctors told me I was lucky. If the knife had been a fraction higher and had sliced into my vertebrae or entered a vital organ, I would have bled to death. As it was, I had lost a great deal of blood. With such a shock to my system, they wanted to keep me in for a few days. They asked for my parents' telephone number but I managed to fob them off by saying they were abroad and instead gave them Gina's. She arrived later that day. So did the police: a middle-aged sergeant with the tired eyes of someone who had seen too much death and violence in his life, and a younger constable. They arrived with their notebooks at the ready, looks of sympathy and endless questions.

'Do you know your attacker?' was their first question.

Fear silenced me. 'No,' I said.

Could I describe the person who had assaulted me? Again I said no.

The nurse saved me. 'That's enough for today,' she said sternly. 'She needs to rest.' But I knew they would be back.

I was right. They returned the following day, but this time I had my story ready for them. I believed that if I gave them Eddie's name he would find me again and his revenge would be much worse. Gina tried to persuade me otherwise, saying that if he was behind bars he couldn't do me further harm. I was too terrified to believe her. I had heard of bail being given and guilty people walking away from what the police believed would be a conviction. I was adamant in my refusal.

'I think someone tried to grab my bag,' I improvised, before they had time to put a question to me.

'And then he stabbed you?'

'That must be what happened,' I replied.

'So, let's get this right, Jackie,' the older one said. 'You were just walking down the street and someone unknown to you stabbed you with a knife – someone you didn't see and didn't speak to?'

'Well, he was behind me, so I couldn't, could I?' I said, thinking that would satisfy him and they would go away.

'Mmm,' he said. 'The passer-by who called the ambulance said he saw you talking to a young black man just before you fell. So, who was that, then?'

'I can't remember. Maybe someone asking directions.'

By their expressions, I knew they were not fooled. They tried to reassure me that if I told them who it was they would find him. It was attempted murder, there was a witness and, if arrested, he would go to prison and I would be safe.

I still didn't believe them. Eddie, I was sure, would find me before they found him. The next time he wouldn't miss. So again I maintained that I couldn't remember who had spoken to me.

They left eventually, but the older one gave me his card.

'Well, Jackie, if you decide to remember any more, give us a ring, OK? Or . . .' he gave me a thoughtful look ' . . . if it turns out to be someone you did know, someone you're frightened of, give me a call as well, all right?'

I was doubly scared then – scared that Gina would want me to leave and scared of Eddie finding out I was alive. Surely he hadn't meant that knife wound simply as a warning.

But she reassured me that he didn't know her name or where she lived. The club only knew her first name, so he couldn't trace her and, anyhow, he, too, would be scared of the police. She was convinced he would leave me alone, but for weeks, I wasn't reassured. I accepted my father's offer of money. I was too frightened to find work as a waitress, which was all I thought I would be offered. I might be seen, and he would come back for me again.

It was Gina who saw the article in the paper.

Eddie had been arrested – more, he had been to court. Large amounts of heroin had been found in his flat, as well as a safe stuffed full of money with traces of drugs on most of the notes. He was also part of a group involved in porn and prostitution. His sentence was ten years. He was off the streets. I wondered if the girls whose lives he had destroyed celebrated their freedom or if, desperate for their next fix, they just went to another man who could supply them with drugs. Sadly, I thought, it was likely to be the latter.

I was determined that my past was behind me and it was time to move on. For the first time in nearly two years, I felt safe.

54

I knew Anna was in love with Gina, but I also knew that she would never do anything about it. I wondered what to do about my own feelings. With every day that passed, I found it increasingly difficult to get Gina out of my head. I found my eyes following her around the flat and I used every excuse I could think of to spend time alone with her.

If my persistence in gaining her attention bothered her, she never showed it. She was the same caring person who had rescued me. In the throes of my first major crush, I saw it as something else. I questioned Anna about where Gina went when she was not in the flat. All Gina ever said, when she was leaving to go out or wasn't coming straight home from work, was that she was meeting a friend. The thought of her being somewhere where I was not, of meeting people I didn't know, began to consume me with jealousy. It was those repeated questions that enabled Anna to put two and two together.

'Jackie,' she said one evening, when we were alone, 'Gina's not . . .' I waited for her to continue. After what seemed a long time she added, '. . . you know, not gay.' She gave me a kindly though penetrating glance.

I felt a hot tide of red suffuse my cheeks. Then a wave of anger swept over me because I had been found out and embarrassed. 'What do you mean?' I retorted. Surely I hadn't been that transparent.

'Jackie, I may be short-sighted but I'm not blind,' replied Anna. 'She likes you – likes you a lot. But not in that way.'

I thought of my friendship with Gina, how she had hugged me when I had completed rehab and how she had encouraged me to leave Eddie. If she wasn't interested in me, what had all that been about?

Anna was just trying to warn me off because she was interested in her, I kept telling myself. But that delusion came to an end when Gina announced she had a new boyfriend she wanted us both to meet. I was desperate, but at least she didn't know how I felt about her. I just thanked my lucky stars I hadn't made a fool of myself by telling her.

That was how I met my husband, Kevin, not a man I loved and certainly not a nice man. He was a friend of Rob's, Gina's boyfriend, and I decided when I met him that he could be my camouflage. I now used the word 'boyfriend' both loosely and often, ignoring the concerned expression on Anna's face. She wasn't fooled when she heard me arrange for Kevin and me to go out in four-somes with Rob and Gina. Thus, however painful it was, I was still able to spend time with Gina.

I managed to keep a smile plastered on my face when I saw Rob's arms round her shoulders. Before I slept with Kevin, I managed to look cheerful when they dropped me off, knowing that Gina would be spending the night with Rob. Gina, believing that any friend of Rob's would be as nice as him, was just happy that, after what I had gone through, I had a boyfriend.

Everything might have been all right – Kevin and I would have eventually broken up and maybe then I would have found someone else with whom to have what I had wanted with Gina – except that I discovered I was pregnant.

How could I have been so stupid? I, who had slept with so many men!

The difference was, I suppose, that I hadn't exactly slept with them. Condoms were used, and as soon as the sex was over, they or I left. There was no waking up in the middle of the night wanting to repeat the act, or a steamy sex session in the early hours when half asleep.

But another factor had entered my life: I had seen Dave again.

'I told you, didn't I,' I said to my therapist, 'that I saw him one more time?'

She nodded, and waited for what was to come next.

'It was four months before my wedding,' I said, 'and in a way he was part of the reason I got married.'

55

Dave had written to me, care of my parents. My father had forwarded the letter. He said he was still in London, he had never left the city, just moved to another area. He told me that he was sorry he had left me, that he hoped I was happy and had sorted my life out. He also explained why he had written.

He was ill, very ill, and he told me what was wrong with him. 'I will understand if you cannot face seeing me again.'

I went to him.

He lived in a small flat on the same type of estate that, the moment he was old enough, he had tried to escape. I rang his doorbell and heard shuffling footsteps. When a feeble voice asked who it was, I told him it was me, Jackie, and asked him to let me in. The bolts that kept the outside world out were drawn back, and for the first time in nearly two years, I was face to face with Dave again.

He stood there, a reed-thin young man in an old man's bent and unsteady body. It was Aids, he had told me in his letter. The drugs he was on had ceased to work.

I phoned the hospital, gave his name, and they told me to bring him in. He was dying, I knew. I also knew how much he had hoped I would come and how he had hung on for as long as possible, waiting for me. A taxi took us to the hospital, and once there I went to the ward where so many young men had spent their last days. The doctors told me it was only a matter of time, but I already knew that. I waited in the visitors' lounge while they settled him in. A boy in there tried to comfort me. He was, I think, no more than eighteen. 'I'm making my will,' he told me, 'saying how I want my funeral done. I've chosen the music – thought I'd get them to play "Burn Baby Burn" when the coffin goes out through the curtains. What do you think?'

I looked at his gaunt face, his emaciated body, and noticed the telltale purple marks under his hospital pyjama jacket. I wanted to cry, ask where his mother was and who was caring for him. Instead I looked into eyes that were sparkling with mischief and gave him what I hoped was my biggest smile. 'Sounds good,' I said. 'That'll get them talking, all right.'

It was he, a boy of eighteen who knew he only had a few days left, who comforted me during the time I spent in the hospital. When he saw me sitting in the lounge smoking a cigarette and nursing plastic cups of foul coffee, he followed me in with unsteady steps.

It took Dave four days to die. Four days when I lied about my life in London; four days when I listened to his painful, rasping breath; four days until both he and I welcomed his death.

His face turned yellow, his eyes dulled and not one hour passed when he was not in pain.

'Can't you give him something?' I asked – and later pleaded.

'No,' I was told. Painkillers would affect his tortured breathing.

Instead, they moved him to a smaller ward and placed an oxygen mask on his face.

'He has the right to live as long as he can,' a nurse told me.

'He has the right to die in peace,' I cried.

But he didn't die in peace.

On the fourth day he stopped breathing, but they resuscitated him.

He has to go in an iron lung, they said.

Then the nurse explained that, for that, he had to have an injection. 'Then he will sleep,' she said.

His eyes begged for it, begged to be released, for he knew what I didn't know then: that he wouldn't wake up.

It was the nurse who told me gently that it was possible he wouldn't regain consciousness. That if I had anything I wanted to say, I needed to speak before the injection was given.

I held his hand and told him I loved him.

'I love you too, Jackie,' he said, his last words before the injection.

He was never put in the iron lung. His heart gave out. I went outside the screens as the crash team went in, heard the activity and then the doctor's unemotional voice stating the hour and minute of his death.

Later they took me into a private room where he lay. He looked young again. I kissed his cheek, and his flesh was cold against my lips.

He was twenty-two years old.

I slept with Kevin that night, which until then I had refused to do. I needed warmth, comfort, but just that first time told me he would never give me either.

Anna was the only person I told about what had happened. Dave was not someone I wanted to share. I kept quiet and carried my grief inside me and that, I guess, was another thing that made me careless.

To add to my misery, Gina announced she was getting married and she and Rob were moving out of London.

Three months later Kevin caught me throwing up in his bathroom.

'Are you fucking pregnant?' he asked, in tones that told me this was not something he considered good news.

I looked at him wretchedly. 'I must be,' I whispered.

His face flushed with anger, as though only one of us was responsible for my condition and that someone was not him.

That was when I said I would go home. My parents would take me in. I was not going to have an abortion and he couldn't make me.

'So, where do your parents live, then?' he asked contemptuously. 'Some bleeding squalid northern council estate, I suppose.'

Pride made me raise my head defiantly and tell him that my father was well off. Why didn't I just keep quiet?

As my words sank in, I went, in Kevin's eyes, from encumbrance to possible financial asset. He didn't mention marriage, not then, just asked me enough questions to start believing that I was telling the truth. Then he checked up on my parents. I discovered later that he'd gone to Companies House to find out just how much my father's business was worth. But he never told me – any more than he divulged that he was aware of my time with

Eddie and that I had been hooked on hard drugs. It was something other than love or decency that motivated him to propose to me.

I knew he didn't love me – he never pretended to – but I wanted the baby. I think after seeing what had happened to Dave and dealing with my feelings for Gina, I also wanted the label 'normal'.

So I accepted.

I was seventeen.

Anna tried to persuade me not to. 'You don't love him, Jackie,' she said. She told me that she was keeping the flat on after Gina was married, that I could stay with her, that she would look after me and help bring the baby up. I had other options, she kept repeating.

She kissed me then.

But she was not the person I wanted – that person whose wedding I had been invited to.

I drew away. She repulsed me with her kindness, her caring, as though that was enough to make me want her.

It wasn't.

I told her that it was no use. I was going to get married. I saw the hurt on her face as the realization registered of how lonely she would be, without either Gina or me.

She's another person I find it hard to talk about. Her name brings back not just memories of loss but of guilt as well – for I was not kind in my refusal to stay with her. I just spurned her friendship without thinking of her feelings. She was too good a person not to have looked after me. I would never have had to pay for her caring with sexual favours. I knew even then that the thought of having

286

a baby in the house, a small person she could shower her love on, and who in turn would love her, was what she wanted.

But I turned my back on her and chose a man who had more interest in my father's money than ever he had in me.

56

I phoned my parents and threw myself on their mercy. My mother was mollified by the fact that the man who had made me pregnant wanted to marry me. It was agreed that I could stay with them until the wedding. A month after I returned home, I was married. I was four months pregnant. My parents paid for the wedding and gave my new husband and me a generous cheque to use as a deposit on a house.

My father didn't like Kevin. I think he sensed that this was not going to be a marriage full of love. 'Jackie,' he said, a week before the wedding, 'you don't have to marry him, you know. We could help with the baby.' But in my head I did. My mother, I knew, didn't want me back in the house and I didn't want my baby growing up in her cold, sterile home as I had.

Shortly after the wedding, which was not the big white one my mother may once have dreamt of but a small ceremony in a register office with a handful of friends present, we moved into a house on the outskirts of London.

Five months later I gave birth to my baby, a healthy eight-pound boy. I loved him from the first moment I saw him.

My marriage was another story – not one I want to dwell on for too long. He was an abusive man, who took out his resentment at having married me with hurtful words and flying fists.

I had managed to stay clear of drugs since rehab, but by the time my son was crawling, I had a relapse. My husband – my ticket to respectability – would have been horrified if I had accused him of being a user. Cocaine wasn't a drug, he said, as he and his friends sniffed it. Well, he might not have considered it as such, but dealers I knew had fewer qualms. First it was Mandies that I purchased, but what I really wanted was the buzz that wrapped me in cotton wool and made the world seem a brighter place. It would take away the physical pain when my husband hit me, and the mental one when he called me a druggie whore. So, wanting it, I found it.

After the birth of my son, he had made no bones about his true feelings for me. 'I knew what you were when I first met you,' he taunted. 'Everyone knew you were one of Eddie's girls. Knew you were trash. So does your old man – that's why he wouldn't cough up enough cash for a decent place for us to live. He didn't think you were worth it.'

That was when I realized why he had married me: the house was in his name. He had paid the minimum deposit; the balance of the cheque had gone into his bank account.

Why then did I not do what my teenage self would have done and walked out? I could have admitted that my marriage was a failure and asked my father for help.

I think the fight had gone out of me.

It took the birth of my daughter to bring it back. He had not wanted another baby. But he should have thought of that when he drunkenly forced himself on me. 'She'll end up like you,' he said, 'a good-for-nothing little whore.' He repeated similar words to the baby lying sleeping in her cot. 'You're going to be a junkie whore, just like your fucking no-good mother,' was what he said. She was six weeks old.

I left. He could keep the house, I said.

I moved back up north; accommodation was cheaper there. I found a house with a garden that I wanted to rent. The next thing I had to make my mind up about was how I was going to support two children and myself. I knew a combination of state handouts and guilt money from my father was not what I wanted.

I decided on escort work. It paid well and the tax man didn't take a large chunk of it. And it was the only thing I knew I was good at.

'OK, Jackie,' said my therapist. 'Let's stop there. I want you to think for a moment. What made the work Eddie forced you to do so different from what you decided to do? Not just then, but also when you were younger.'

'When I was twelve,' I said, 'it made me feel good that I could buy whatever I wanted. And when I made those friends, that I could pay for my own drugs and drink.

'But it wasn't just the money. It was more about the control. When I first had sex with that friend of my father's, I felt it was me who controlled him. So, to a certain extent, it was about power. When I was in that car and saw the expression on his face, I just knew he wanted me. His hands were almost trembling on the steering-wheel.

He could hardly meet my gaze and that made me feel powerful.

'I had been controlled for so long and I felt then that it was my turn. In my twenties, I felt the same.

'And,' I said to her, 'I'll tell you something. A lot of men out there like to be controlled. They like pain and being humiliated, and I found them.'

'You mean you became a dominatrix?'

'Yes, that's exactly what I was.'

57

As far as I was concerned, my life was sorted. I was only in my twenties and earning more money than I had ever dreamt about. I was able to send my son to a private junior school and have an au pair living in who babysat when I was out working.

Once again, I had a wardrobe of nice clothes, only this time I had paid for them myself, plus I had plenty of money in the bank. I planned to buy a house, then another to rent out. In a few years I could retire, I thought. I'd be financially secure. Maybe buy a small wine bar, give myself something to do.

But the one thing I was determined not to do was get emotionally entangled. I had affairs with women, nice affectionate ones, but nothing too deep. Men were solely business.

'What changed?' asked my therapist.

'I met Helena – believe it or not in a music venue, in Manchester, though, not London. It might sound corny to say our eyes met across a crowded bar, but that's exactly what happened.'

She nodded, and I told her the final part of my story.

I saw a slim girl, dressed casually in jeans and a loose sweater. Her hair was straight and glossy, her skin smooth and her eyes, when I caught her gaze, were brown. Not the brown so dark that little of their expression is evident, but the soft colour of a creamy caramel toffee. Those warm eyes smiled at me and, picking up my drink, I moved over to where she was sitting.

That night, we talked incessantly, as if we had known each other all our lives. I was oblivious to everyone else around me and I knew I must see her again. I asked for her phone number and telephoned early the following morning. 'I want to see you,' I said.

We met in a small, cosy wine bar where she told me she had taken a degree course at Leeds University and was now working for Social Services.

She asked me what I did – which, that night, I brushed off. I said something about being between jobs, which, although partly true, gave little away as to what my profession was.

I already knew that I didn't want to walk away from her.

I told her the truth before we went to bed for the first time. I felt I had to – I owed her that. Then, without meaning to, I told her everything else. We talked – or, rather, I talked and she listened into the early hours of the morning.

Afterwards, when I was finally drained of all emotion, she took my hand and led me to the bedroom.

That was when, for the very first time, I discovered the difference between making love and just having sex. It was more, much more, than two bodies entwined: it was the touching of fingers, toes, mouths and faces; it was the wanting to merge with her, to be held, and wanting never to let go.

It was loving the scent of her, the feel of softness and the sound of her voice. When we were together, I could feel her skin against mine even when we weren't touching. Each time I saw her I felt breathless with a happiness I had never believed possible.

'Jackie,' she said, some time after we had met, 'where do you see our relationship going?'

I couldn't answer that question easily. All I knew was that I wanted to be with her and said so.

She told me then that she couldn't handle me being an escort. 'I know I don't have the right to tell you how to live your life, but that's the way I feel,' she said. She told me she understood why I might think that was all I could do, but she insisted it wasn't.

She asked if I was using again and I admitted I was. That was another condition: I had to get clean.

That night I sat and thought through my options. I could be an escort with plenty of money and take the drugs I wanted. My other choice was to have a relationship that made me happy, not have much money and put myself through rehab again.

I chose the second option.

Rehab was no better that time round than it had been before; the only difference was, I knew what to expect – and I had Helena for support.

After that, with my sporadic education, I knew if I was going to do more than stand behind a bar, hoping my mental arithmetic was good enough to add up a bill, or work as a waitress, I had to rethink.

'Evening classes. Lots of adults do them,' said Helena.

So I said goodbye to leather skirts, black stockings, suspenders, push-up bras and low-cut tops. Instead, I put on jeans and a sweatshirt and enrolled in adult literacy classes.

A year later we moved in together. I bought the house I had planned to. I was unable to pay cash for it, but I had saved enough for a respectable deposit. My divorce from

Kevin went through smoothly. I let him keep my share of the proceeds of the house sale, and that was enough for him not to contest it.

Some time after that Helena and I decided we wanted more than just living together and decided to get married. First, I broke the news to my parents. I expected screams of outrage from my mother – after all, she was of a different generation – but that was not what happened. She said she was happy for me, that two grandchildren were enough and, anyhow, she had never liked Kevin. Even his name was common. Well, some things never change, and 'Helena', I had to admit, did sound classier. My mother actually agreed to look after my daughter when we went on honeymoon, and my son went to stay with friends.

My father seemed a bit startled, but took it in his stride. Now he had two daughters, he said, and really that was his only comment on the matter.

Next I had to tell my children. Nervously I sat them down and explained. My son said, 'Cool, Mum,' and my daughter, 'Awesome.'

The only blot on my life was that, without drugs, my five-year-old self was making her appearance again. Helena told me it didn't matter, that she could deal with it, but I decided, once the wedding was over, I needed to seek professional help.

My therapist smiled. 'Tell me about the wedding, Jackie.'

It was a perfect day, the best day of my life.

Helena looked wonderful, all shiny hair and sparkling big brown eyes. She was wearing a white strappy top, black trousers and high-heeled boots that reminded me of the ones I had once worn.

We had planned everything together, the hotel for the reception, the menu and the flowers. Not wanting the normal cheesy wedding music, we even took along CDs of our choice. As people arrived, we had the slow version of Cascada singing 'Everytime We Touch', and walked in to Aerosmith's 'I Don't Wanna Miss A Thing'. As we signed the register we had Bon Jovi's 'Thank You For Loving Me' played, and finally we walked out to the sounds of Savage Garden's 'Truly Madly Deeply'.

We then went to a large hotel in Manchester where a buffet had been laid on for us and our guests. Later we cut the three-tier chocolate cake.

We had hired a DJ for the evening and told him not to play anything too 'different'. 'I want my parents to like it as well, so stick to standards,' I told him. Yes, that's right, my parents were there. So were my son and daughter.

The champagne flowed, faces beamed, my parents chatted to Helena's, music played and we literally danced the night away.

Once the last guest had gone, Helena and I spent the night together in the presidential suite and, the following morning, flew to Toronto for our honeymoon. It was such a beautiful city. We hired bikes and explored as much of it as we could. We spent a day wandering round the grounds of the Casa Loma, ate a meal at the top of CN Tower and finally took a boat trip to the Niagara Falls. Then we came home.

That was the end of my story, and the beginning of one that I have yet to live. One that I know will be happy. The only thing I had to deal with was the visits from my younger self.

'Why?' I asked my therapist. 'Why now, when I'm happy? What is it she wants? That's what I would like to ask her.'

'I think,' my therapist said, 'that she wants to know if you're still angry with her. When she has been reassured enough, I think you'll find she'll go. Jackie,' she asked me then, 'how do you feel about her now?'

'I feel sad,' I said, 'when I think of the little girl I once was and what those men did to her. I don't think she stood a chance, do you?'

'No,' said my therapist, 'she didn't – but the adult you does.'

After my early sessions, my therapist talked to Helena; she told her how to handle the appearance of my younger self. The most important thing was to make the little girl feel safe.

We bought soft toys that Helena gave her, when she came. To begin with, there were times when an ambulance had to be called – that was when the little girl was angry and frightened. But gradually she appeared more content. Helena said my other self was rather sweet and just wanted to play.

She comes much less now.

'Will I ever be completely better?' I asked my therapist, when my sessions were drawing to an end.

'What do you think, Jackie?' she asked.

'Not completely,' I said.

58

Over the time I had been seeing her, my therapist had told me to get rid of some of my hurt and anger by writing letters to the people who had harmed me. They were never sent – I had no address for most of them.

I wrote to my parents and told them what I thought of their neglect, of how they never noticed that as a small child I had become disturbed. I spoke to my mother only through those letters. Spoke to her of her selfishness, her lack of caring and how she had put her social life before me. I wrote of the anger I felt towards her, and of how as a mother she had let me down. To my father I said I knew that in his own way he had done his best. He had tried on that holiday in Spain, even if he had failed to love me. Those letters covered the root causes of my feelings from small child to adult. That was one pile.

I wrote to others as well, to those I had met along the way, but the biggest pile was to my uncle.

In them I wrote of how he had destroyed my life. That he was the worst sort of pervert. I pulled no punches. But it was my final letter to him that I took to my therapist. Even though our sessions had stopped, I wanted her to see it. I'd written it after he had had his stroke.

Did you wonder why the doctors have given you so many drugs to make you sleep? Did you wonder, too, why the nurses looked at you coldly? I think you did or maybe you knew before I visited you. I told you then, did I not? Told you what I had done: that I had made up my mind that you were never going to return to your home. That I had gone to the doctor, the one in charge of the hospital, told him I was worried that the ward you were in was so near the children's one. Oh, I know you couldn't walk then, but you might have learnt again, mightn't you?

Were you a danger? Well, we both know: not to the children on that ward. But you were to me, to my peace of mind. For every day that I know you live is another day when my past haunts me. Once I had returned to the north, you were at all the family parties, in photographs that were shown around, a name on people's lips. And I wanted you gone.

The stroke you had. If only you hadn't been found so fast, you wouldn't have recovered. But you were, and then they rushed you into hospital.

But you do remember my visit? I only came once. And remember what I whispered in your ear: that there is another hospital they will send you to; one where evil old men are put.

You believed me, believed every word I said. You looked at me so pleadingly for you no longer had the power of speech. Your hand grasped the blanket and I knew from its faint movements that you wanted to stretch it out to me, but you didn't have the strength.

A little trickle of saliva ran down your chin. It was so disgusting! It repelled me. I left you then. I had nothing more to say.

That night the phone call came. It was from my mother and she was crying: you were her big brother.

I went with her to see you lying there. You were bruised, you know. Those doctors had tried to pull you back from the dead. They had run electric shocks through your body, trying to jump-start that evil heart of yours.

But you didn't want to come back, did you? I'd made sure of that.

I went to the crematorium and watched as your coffin went through that curtain. I said goodbye as I imagined the flames consuming your body. I had a drink later. I raised a glass when the guests raised theirs. 'To his memory,' they said.

Oh, yes, Uncle, I remember you well.

'Is that really what you did, Jackie?' she asked, and I knew she wanted to find out if this was just a picture superimposed over a different event, or if it was true.

'What do you think?' I asked.

We smiled at each other with understanding.

Then I left, and went to where Helena and my children were waiting.